PUBLIC SCHOOLED

A NOVEL

JOHN FENIMORE

ISBN: 1468167715
ISBN 13: 9781468167719

DEDICATION

To the classroom teacher

PUBLIC SCHOOLED – A NOVEL

Prologue   **Orientation**   ix

Part 1 Marking period one   1

Chapter 1   The supervisor   3
Chapter 2   The assistant superintendent   17
Chapter 3   The new guy   29
Chapter 4   The interview committee   39
Chapter 5   The acting superintendent   49
Chapter 6   The mayor's office   59
Chapter 7   The union boss   65
Chapter 8   The principals   73
Chapter 9   The board of education   81

Part 2 Marking period 2   91

Chapter 10   The supervisor   93
Chapter 11   The assistant superintendent   105
Chapter 12   The new guy   113
Chapter 13   The interview committee   127
Chapter 14   The acting superintendent   135
Chapter 15   The mayor's office   153
Chapter 16   The union boss   163
Chapter 17   The principals   173
Chapter 18   The board of education   181

Part 3 Marking period 3   **191**

Chapter 19   The supervisor   193
Chapter 20   The assistant superintendent   199
Chapter 21   The new guy   207
Chapter 22   The interview committee   217
Chapter 23   The acting superintendent   223
Chapter 24   The mayor's office   231
Chapter 25   The union boss   235
Chapter 26   The principals   241
Chapter 27   The board of education   247

Part 4 Marking period 4   **253**

Chapter 28   The supervisor   255
Chapter 29   The assistant superintendent   261
Chapter 30   The new guy   269
Chapter 31   The interview committee   275
Chapter 32   The acting superintendent   279
Chapter 33   The mayor's office   287
Chapter 34   The union boss   291
Chapter 35   The principals   297
Chapter 36   The board of education   303

Epilogue   **Graduation**   **315**

List of Characters   **322**

PROLOGUE
ORIENTATION

PROLOGUE

ORIENTATION

Thirty minutes earlier, the old, tired auditorium rocked with excitement. The poorly lit room had been filled with anxious teachers wearing red t-shirts, worried parents wondering about budget cuts, and retired citizens convinced schools primarily existed to cushion its workers from the real world, offering nothing more to society than burdensome taxes. When the meeting first began, a citizen filled every seat, and additional people stood, lining the side aisles and back of the room like those who arrived at church too late on Christmas morning.

Attempting to begin the second half of the meeting, Board president Larry Griffiths tried to get order by banging his gavel, a practice for which his dislike matched his ineffectiveness, and the audience continued to ignore him. Two security guards stood by helplessly, like a first-year teachers trying to calm a study hall packed with twelfth graders ready to tear down the walls on a sweltering June afternoon.

Many in the audience had gone home after the break separating the public portion of the meeting and the business portion. The Board of Education meeting continued as those remaining finally settled into their seats. The Board needed to vote on whether or not to offer the Acting

Superintendent a new contract. A proposal had just been voted on whether or not to vote for the new contract at this moment of the meeting. The proposal confused a few members of the Board. After the proposal on whether or not to take a vote had passed unanimously, one of the newest Board members raised her hand.

"What did we just vote on?" Laura Benderman asked.

Board president Griffiths answered, "Uh, we just voted to vote on Mr. DelVecchio's new contract."

"But of course we have to vote on it," she stated. "Mr. DelVecchio's contract ends in ten days. We have to make a decision."

"Wait a minute," interrupted long-time Board member Vito Viterelli. 'I didn't know that's what we were voting on."

"Maybe we should re-vote," Board president Griffiths offered.

The remaining crowd in the audience simultaneously groaned and roared with rude laughter.

High school English teacher Leonia Calabrese, attending her first Board meeting ever, though she had worked in the district for fifteen years, turned to a colleague seated next to her. "Just what the fuck goes on in central office all day anyway?" she asked in wonderment.

PART 1
FIRST MARKING PERIOD

ONE

THE SUPERVISOR

"Your parents are dead."

Lucy, five years old, stared silently at her grief-stricken grandmother as the older woman, her face even with Lucy's, quietly but firmly spoke the words as she knelt in front of the little girl.

Lucy blinked twice, saying nothing.

She had been dropped off at Grandma Irene's while her parents attended the ballet in the city. The couple was killed in a two-car accident going through the tunnel as they returned to retrieve young Lucy. The arrival never occurred. Lucy was alone. As an only child, Lucy hated when her parents left her with Grandma Irene, her maternal grandmother, whose entire house smelled of lilac toilet water or on some occasions, Evening in Paris. After her parents' deaths, young Lucy sometimes awakened in the morning uncertain of her whereabouts. She would shiver and hide under the covers of the bed. This developed even further into a constant fear of being left alone.

Grandma Irene, a gray haired and squarely built widow, was sixty years old when Lucy was born. Lucy may have been raised by Grandma Irene, but for much of the time the girl entertained herself while Irene offered private instruction to other young children whose parents hoped and vainly dreamed of Van Cliburn or even Amy Beach-type success at the piano. Grandma insisted that during lessons Lucy stay silent and invisible.

The broken notes and oft-repeated errors sounded throughout the small house while Lucy stayed out of sight reading Grandma Irene's classic novels, looking at her large picture books of exotic places, or drawing pictures of a fantasized family consisting of a father, a mother, and two children standing in front of a modest house surrounded by a pure white picket fence.

When Lucy entered tenth grade, she attracted the attention of a recently graduated young man, smart, ambitious, and the owner of a new red Chevy Camaro convertible. The now blossoming blue-eyed beauty had been impressed both with the automobile and the fact that a boy old enough to drive and own a car had shown an interest in her. The young man had gotten a job right after high school and had money to spend on his young girlfriend. Of average height, with appropriately long hair and sideburns for the time, and he enjoyed cruising around town with Lucy in tow.

The young man knew he had a future beauty on his hands, and he knew he had better control Lucy, as future competition, from smarter, wealthier, and better looking young men would soon discover her.

He gave Lucy orders and she followed. She would be not abandoned again.

"Make me a sandwich, and I will take you for a ride," he would say, knowing how much Lucy loved the feeling of protection afforded in the shiny red car as it passed her 10th grade classmates, walking in groups of three or four along the sidewalk. She would turn her face and hide from them, however, fearing anyone's frowns and stares.

Lucy, the lonely little girl without parents, preferred to remain silent and invisible, just as she had while Grandma Irene gave piano lessons in her little house years ago.

If Lucy spoke up, the boyfriend would say sternly, "Don't get too big for your britches, Lucy, or you will be walking. Alone. You know the other girls don't like you much anyway because you can be such a bitch."

"I am sorry," Lucy would say immediately, looking down at her feet.

Her parents' deaths had left her feeling abandoned and without steady guidance. Grandma Irene tried her best, but someone born in the last decade of the nineteenth century certainly could not understand how to raise a teenager in the late 1960s. Lucy counted on her boyfriend more and more.

He continued to tell her what to do and she did it. He scolded her and she would try to make him happy. They married three years after she graduated high school, while she attended her third year at the local commuter college. The young man did not deter her as she pursued her education. Her classes and homework kept him free for his own pursuits.

Lucy, however, possessed a silent and unspoken determination: she would have her own career as an elementary teacher, she would make a reality the fantasized family of four in the house surrounded by the white picket fence, and she would be determined to keep that family and marriage intact. She would not feel abandoned again.

She often tried to hide her radiant beauty to avoid attention. When she completed her student teaching in the Menlo Grove school district, her principal recommended her to another principal in the district. Her empathy for children and her talent working a classroom were apparent.

The first principal, an older man who Lucy saw as a father figure overseeing her early progress as a teacher, called his colleague across town.

"Hire her," he said. "She's a good teacher. And she's got great legs."

Lucy arrived for new teacher orientation appropriately dressed for the mid-1970s: short plaid skirt, white blouse, green eye shadow, and a blue blazer. She always wore a blazer or a jacket. A secretary gave her a nametag to wear on the jacket pocket of the blazer.

The vice-principal, an aging former basketball coach in the district, greeted each of the first-year teachers individually. When he came to Lucy, he leaned close to her face, and looked directly down at her nametag, his face not six inches away from her bosom.

"Ah, Lucy," he said, reading her name tag, "and what do you call the other one?"

The color drained from Lucy's face. She refused to let such comments or attitudes deter her. She was determined to teach young children, and in her classroom they would learn to read, to enjoy writing, and to feel safe.

She looked down at her feet and said nothing as the V.P. chuckled to himself and moved on to the next novice.

She had already dealt with plenty. She could deal with clueless men. "Everyone has to learn to cope with what life," she thought.

With her first paycheck she purchased outfits that covered her figure and made her look older than her years. This habit would continue throughout her career. But in her second grade classroom she possessed masterful technical skills. And the children in her room were under her spell.

The little boys loved with her. And the little girls wanted to be her.

While her career continued and her successes in the classroom accumulated, the criticism and the control at home continued as well.

"When do we eat?" her husband grumbled.

"I just got home," Lucy replied in exasperation. "I had a faculty meeting after school, and then I stopped at the grocery store to get some food. Maybe you could help once in a while."

"Oh, cut it out," he sarcastically said. "You're a school teacher, for God's sake. Try getting a real job and then we'll talk about helping out."

Lucy closed her eyes and bit er tongue while she began unpacking the groceries.

She eventually received recognition as teacher of the year. But as the years passed and her career continued on a trajectory upward, her husband's career began to founder. His small business began losing money to overseas manufacturing and his own extravagant lifestyle. The red Camaro eventually replaced by larger, more expensive, showier automobiles, oversized houses with swimming pools, extravagant and frequent vacations, boats, and exorbitantly priced season tickets to professional sports teams.

The loss of income eventually transformed his once successful business and gregarious personality into mere facades. Public servant Lucy's steady income increased as her husband's decreased. However, Lucy continued her usual silence as her husband's insulting remarks continued regarding her conservative clothing or any weight gain.

Lucy also became responsible for paying more and more of the bills that arrived with the regularity of school marking periods. Two children arrived to brighten the home, but the couple continued deeper and deeper into debt. The plane was sold, the cars fell into disrepair, and the large home aged gracelessly. The husband began spending more and more hours away from home, but with less and less money arriving from the business. Lucy continued preparing dinner every evening after she had arrived home from school and her long commute and picking up the kids from day care.

After she cleaned up after dinner, she would pull multiple piles of papers from her school bag and begin the process of reviewing student work and then making adjustments to the next day's lessons.

"Are you going to spend all night again doing school work?" he loudly asked.

"I have to review these students' papers to see which kids are understanding what's going on in class and which are still confused," she would even more loudly reply. "Why don't you seem to get that?"

The door slammed as he left the house, leaving behind a trail of indecipherable sarcasm, with only the word "shrew" discernable to Lucy's ears. He frequently would come home from work later and later. Sometimes he didn't come home at all. Lucy began to feel invisible in her own house. The children were raised, educated, grew into young adults, and moved out.

Lucy's current position, late in her career, as elementary supervisor meant her office was located in the central administration building. She worked with ten other district supervisors, those former teachers who had moved from classroom teachers to become the trainers, overseers, and evaluators of teachers. The "academic" content supervisors - English, Math, Science, and Social Studies - stayed housed in one of the four middle schools or two high schools in the district.

Supervisors served as experts in their content area. Building principals counted on the supervisors to help in running the building: assisting on lunch room duty if necessary, standing in the hallways as students passed to limit rowdiness and bullying, organizing and implementing the state testing, and keeping the building principal informed of any classroom issues in case a parent was to call the principal with a complaint regarding a teacher.

Many principals would state the obvious if pressed: they would rather live without assistant principals than live without supervisors. A supervisor could help run a building better than an assistant principal could help run curriculum. In truth, principals could not run their buildings well without either.

Now, many years later, the events of her past remained part of Lucy Williams, standing outside her office in the central administration building as she prepared to begin another school year

She observed a new guy, Michael Ferrone, soon-to-be hired central office administrator, walk past her in the hallway on his way to his final interview with the Acting Superintendent. He hadn't even bothered to acknowledge her existence. Lucy's goal of appearing invisible was apparently working.

Lucy rolled her eyes after Ferrone passed.

The district's testing coordinator, Brenda Dredahl, middle aged, single, tall and gangly with oversized feet and long, stringy hair, had been part of the initial interview committee for Michael Ferrone, the latest Assistant Superintendent, who had just blithely ignored Lucy Williams standing outside her office.

Brenda approached and whispered to Lucy, "There's your new boss," as the thin, middle-aged man about Lucy's age walked up the hallway to meet the Acting Superintendent of the Menlo Grove.

The new Assistant Superintendent came from outside the district, an unusual move for Menlo Grove, as incestuous a public school district as existed in the state. Tall and fit, the dark suit fit the new guy well. His black shoes shined like sunshine hitting chrome.

"What does he know about elementary?' Lucy asked Brenda.

"Probably not much. Former high school teacher and coach, recently a supervisor."

"Oh, really," Lucy said sarcastically. "Another high school guy." Lucy groaned as she rolled her eyes again.

Elementary instruction was Lucy's bulwark, and she protected it. The new guy appeared to be just another in a long line of high school people who obtained central office jobs, just another guy to answer to, just another administrator with no knowledge of the mysteries or nuances of young learners.

Lucy knew what that meant. The current Assistant Superintendent of Curriculum and Instruction, Lilly Laboy, had also come from a high school background, and although Lilly had served as a middle school principal, she had little patience for elementary school issues.

Lilly's most common expression to Lucy and the elementary principals of the large district was, "It's not rocket science. For Christ's sake, it's fucking ELEMENTARY school!"

Lilly Laboy's attitude toward elementary education shook Lucy's core. She had devoted her 35-year career, minus the two years she had taken off to have her two children, to learning the intricacies of the elementary classroom. Twenty-five years as a teacher, then five more as a classroom specialist - training non-tenured teachers -and now the elementary supervisor of the ten elementary school buildings in the school district. All this experience had molded her into an expert in elementary classroom instruction. No one in the district knew more about early literacy than Lucy Williams.

She had been afforded little credit in her achievements, however, from some of her former colleagues. Three of these colleagues had gone into administration as elementary principals, and these three fought Lucy in a constant and uneasy struggle to move the district's elementary curriculum into a unified model.

The three principals were determined to keep their own thumbs on their respective building's programs, and out of the hands of Lucy, their work colleague and Friday afternoon drinking partner when they all were beginning their careers many years ago as young teachers.

They had all worked together as classroom specialists after leaving the classroom, helping young teachers learn the intricacies of running a classroom and delivering instruction in an effective way. They had been close as teachers can be. Only another classroom teacher knows the difficulty of the job or the long-term relationships that often result.

The women did have two things in common, however. The first was their passion about Menlo Grove's children.

The second was how they had become the primary breadwinners in their households as their husbands, all talented and well-compensated employees in their own careers, saw those careers downsized, outsourced, and suddenly found themselves middle-aged, part-timed, unemployed, or unemployable. What effect this had on each marriage proved difficult to measure, even to those within the marriage.

Once Lucy became a supervisor and began evaluating teachers, she observed the vast difference in style and competence of the instructors in the classrooms. Each month on a Friday a different elementary principal would host the other principals for a lunch meeting in her respective school and share common concerns. Lucy would be invited. Often, however, these lunch meetings turned into whining sessions containing mostly moaning, groaning, and complaining.

Lucy would try to move the conversation to the varied classroom competencies she observed in the ten different buildings.

"I have seen so much variation in talent, so much variation in curriculum being taught," Lucy declared at one of the meetings.

"We are all in different buildings; we all have different needs and concerns," retorted Barbara Jean Cox, one of the principals. "Not having ever been a principal, Lucy, you wouldn't understand."

"But I have seen teachers in every building," Lucy replied. "As principals you only know what is going on in your own building. I believe some of your teachers haven't even looked at their curriculum guides. I have written those guides and trained teachers on how to use them. Why aren't all your teachers using the district curriculum as it is written?"

Cyndi Zubricki broke into the conversation. "Barbara Jean is right. Every one of our building needs is different. We know what our students need."

"But we are one district," Lucy replied. "We only have one curriculum."

"With all due respect," Rosemary Grogan-Unangst said, "I have to agree with Barbara Jean and Cyndi. This is a big town. Our students come from many different backgrounds and have different needs. We cannot be tied to a single curriculum. It's simply too limiting."

Lucy now considered the three women principals her former friends, and "she-wolves."

"I know more than anyone in this district does about elementary curriculum," one of the three she-wolves, Barbara Jean Cox, would say directly, her diminutive stature belying the size of her mouth.

Lucy eventually decided it pointless to continue returning fire, instead relegated to sit looking down at her feet. Eventually the invitations to Lucy to attend these elementary principal luncheons ceased. Lucy did not mind missing the monthly abuse.

The fact that Acting Superintendent Michael DelVecchio had given the three "she-wolves" his personal cell phone number, and the fact that they each called him several times every day, made certain Lucy's influence was kept limited despite her expertise.

The three principals also had seniority and control over most of the other seven elementary principals. The three made certain they had a hand in choosing every new principal in the district. They made certain of every other elementary principal's awareness regarding the power the three had with DelVecchio because of their personal and political connections with him and within the sprawling district.

But all principals expend the bulk of their time and energy keeping a building running smoothly. Therefore, despite the personal undermining of the three she-wolves, Lucy had made serious progress with the elementary curriculum. She had built a solid career just as she had been determined to do, just as she had built her family and kept her marriage together.

Lucy, as the elementary supervisor, tried to keep her distance from school politics, having no interest in anything more than the sequential development of young minds. Lucy also knew that Lilly Laboy had control of the actual academic workings of the district. DelVecchio, meanwhile, would continue count on Lilly Laboy to keep the division of Curriculum and Instruction running smoothly and keep a check on the new guy, under the aegis of "teaching him the job."

Lilly would be taking over the Student Services division, the cottage industry of every school district in the state, the one that grew larger and larger, and consumed more and more dollars of the budget each year. Lilly, as Assistant Superintendent of Student Services with a silent but powerful hand remaining in Curriculum & Instruction, would now control virtually all the money devoted to both general and special education.

Lucy Williams realized that Lily Laboy had reached the pinnacle of her power as an educator.

Lucy wondered, though, how new guy Ferrone would manage to run Curriculum and Instruction without the access to DelVecchio's ear that Lilly possessed, and with Lilly controlling the purse strings.

"Responsibility without authority. Good luck, buddy," Lucy thought to herself, still somewhat annoyed new guy Ferrone had not noticed her in the hallway.

The larger problem looming for both DelVecchio and Lilly that Lucy Williams did not recognize would be next spring's Board election, and keeping the three incumbent Board of Education members in office. Their reelection would determine Michael and Lilly's focus over the next year, even more so than curriculum, instruction, or student services.

DelVecchio's contract was set to expire at the conclusion of this school year next June 30. Therefore, his primary goal right now was getting a new contract. The Board of Education election next April would determine who would be sitting in judgment of the Acting Superintendent's future.

So while Lucy the supervisor concentrated on trying to implement a common curriculum for all the elementary schools, what she failed to understand was that the Board election next spring would determine the professional futures of Michael DelVecchio and Lilly Laboy. And, although she didn't realize it at the moment, next spring would also determine the future of Lucy the elementary supervisor as well.

TWO

THE ASSISTANT SUPERINTENDENT

Lilly Laboy had moved from high school English teacher to department supervisor to middle school principal to Assistant Superintendent through a combination of intelligence, inexhaustible work ethic, and most importantly, her fierce loyalty to Michael DelVecchio, the Acting Superintendent.

Tiny physically, almost emaciated, her clothes, which hung on her bony physique, resembled thrift-shop leftovers from a hippie fest. Her blond hair, streaked with gray, was curly, unruly, and looked like it had just exploded. Lilly would stick a pencil in her hair as she rapidly spoke with both hands gesturing wildly. One could tell how harried Lilly's day had been by the number of writing utensils sticking out of her hair.

Though small in stature, she appeared much larger when she entered a room or conducted a meeting. Lilly, in her new position as Assistant Superintendent of Student Services, would be kept busy handling lawsuits, dysfunctional child study team members, and parents of the disabled learners. Nevertheless, her greatest challenge was keeping DelVecchio in his position past his current contract, due to expire at the end of the school year.

She had DelVecchio, all the building administrators, including the three "she-wolf" elementary principals, and all the supervisors, including Lucy, in her control, as they all feared her tenaciousness. Once, Cyndi Zubricki, one of the she-wolves, felt Lilly's wrath in front of a roomful of administrators.

"Parents will no longer be allowed to drop off a kid after school has begun, " Lilly announced to the gathering of building principals. "From now on anyone arriving at school even one minute late must have a parent sign them in to the main office."

Cyndi tried to protest. "I am not sure that will work in my building," she began.

"It WILL work in EVERYONE'S building," Lilly shouted. "It is YOUR job as a building principal to MAKE it work," she said coldly, staring directly at Cyndi.

"When I was a building principal," she continued as those in the room rolled their eyes en masse, "this procedure worked for me, and you will make it work for you."

She-wolf principal Cyndi Zubricki decided to take a Xanex the moment she returned to her office.

Most of the principals, highly skilled building managers, were actually more interested in education than acquiring power anyway. They let Lilly have her say and did as they were told just to keep her out of their building.

The principals, especially the three elementary she-wolves, knew the new Assistant Superintendent, or "the new guy," as they would call him, could easily be kept in his place by Lilly. She simply would ignore any of his ideas to develop the district's lack of a cohesive plan for curriculum if those ideas upset the current order, or more importantly, could hurt DelVecchio politically.

With no tenure protection for three full years, the new guy could be sent packing for any reason at all if he didn't fall into step. No, Lilly would not concern herself with him. Her control of the district continued to grow. Keeping DelVecchio in his position after the next BOE election was her primary goal to continuing her control and influence in the district.

For all her control at central office, however, Lilly's personal life was more complicated. Married for twenty-five years to the same man, Lilly had little sway over her spouse's behavior. In fact, she had married a school principal in the Menlo Grove district when she was still a classroom teacher, and the man she married was a control freak who had trouble controlling himself.

Lilly's husband, Charles Laboy, seemed to possess the misguided idea that if he could sleep with as many of the female administrators in the district as were willing, he could control and manipulate them as he did Lilly.

He was slight of build, with dark, powerful eyebrows and a nearly perfect profile. His dark penetrating eyes had melted many female educators over the years. In the bars after work on Fridays, teachers would congregate to replace the smell of school children with the smell of beer, vodka, and apricot brandy. Charles Laboy proved especially effective in this setting.

On his way to accomplishing his improbable and vain goal of bedding as many female principals of the district as possible, one of the affairs went sour, and one particular principal, looking to salvage her own marriage, reported Charles's inappropriate behavior to Claire Smith, the previous Superintendent, claiming sexual harassment.

Superintendent Smith had already shaken up the district by not only becoming the first female to hold the superintendency in the history of the Menlo Grove school district, but by shaking up the old boys' club for which Menlo Grove was so well known. She ruled strongly, and would actually listen to the women of the district, a rare practice here.

By state law, Smith was required to report the harassment allegation to the Affirmative Action Officer in the district. This responsibility formerly was held by the then Director of Human Resources, Michael DelVecchio, but Claire, upon being appointed Superintendent, appointed a new Affirmative Action officer, and DelVecchio had this responsibility removed.

The new Affirmative Action Officer also happened to be Assistant Superintendent of Curriculum and Instruction, Lilly Laboy. Although Lilly certainly could not investigate her own husband, Superintendent Smith informed Lilly of the charge. Lilly may have moved the job to the current Assistant Superintendent of Student Services, but the damage had been done to both Lilly and Charles.

This situation proved to be the end of Charles's official career in public education, though his marriage to Lilly survived. Charles was forced to take early retirement at the age of 52, and managed to survive quite well with the state's generous teachers' pension, figured at more than 60% of his highest three years' salaries. With the addition of Lily's $150,000 annual salary as Assistant Superintendent, Charles and Lily managed to purchase a second home at the southernmost end of the Shore.

The settlement agreement with the district also allowed Charles to return to the district annually for a month each fall to assist in mentoring new principals at a per diem rate of $600.

Despite the humiliation of her husband's cheating, his controlling behavior, and the embarrassing conclusion to his otherwise successful career in public education, Lilly managed to maintain and expand her circle of power. Her current motivation was fed daily by the determination for independence she felt after every phone call from Charles, who rang her cell phone several times each day. He would call in the morning to find out what time Lily arrived at work, call again in late morning to check with whom she would be eating lunch (Lilly usually skipped lunch), and three or four times during the afternoon to determine what time she would be leaving for home.

The position and responsibilities Lilly had in the district usually meant ten-hour days at the minimum. Meetings in DelVecchio's office usually began when central office cleared out at 4:00 P.M., and meetings with community leaders, union officials, or Board members seldom began before 7:00 P.M. Truth be told, Lilly was in no hurry to rush home to Charles anyway.

Today's meeting with Acting Superintendent Michael DelVecchio would focus on the new Assistant Superintendent, the upcoming building referendum, and, of course, the next BOE election.

"So," Lilly began, "what did you think of the new guy?"

"If you think he can do the job, so do I," DelVecchio replied.

"Did you call his references?" Lilly asked.

"I called one of them," Michael said, smiling broadly. "Remember, I am still serving as Director of Human Resources."

"Of course," Lilly grinned, recalling DelVecchio's sudden rise last year from H.R. to Acting Superintendent. He had agreed to keep the old job in human resources while taking on his new role of leading the district as acting superintendent "to save the taxpayers of Menlo Grove money" since the ousted superintendent was still under contract and would have to be paid the remainder of her salary for the next eighteen months – more than $300,000 to stay home.

Point of fact, DelVecchio had little time for his old job. His H.R. secretaries did all his work, mostly tracking resumes and checking on certifications. The yearly state reports consisted mainly of copying and pasting numbers. He was paid a stipend of $10,000 to maintain his previous responsibilities.

"I called one of his former principals,' DelVecchio continued. "She went to Henry Ford High School in this district back in the day while I was the head football coach."

"And P.E. chairman," Lilly reminded him of his former academic role.

"Whatever," Michael said.

"Ferrone's former principal couldn't speak highly enough of the guy. Smart, innovative, honest. The complete package, according to her."

"Hope he doesn't try to be too innovative," Lucy interjected.

"I hope he doesn't try to be too honest," smiled DelVecchio grimly.

"He'll be fine," Lilly concluded. "I'll have a meeting so the principals and supervisors can meet him. He presents himself well. He's articulate. He has solid curriculum credentials and is a former supervisor, so the supervisors should like him."

"Whatever," said DelVecchio, glancing at the morning's local newspaper.

Lilly continued, "His previous employers wrote glowing letters of reference for him, so I think the principals will take to him. Anyway, I hope."

"The principals report to me, not the new guy," Michael stated firmly. "Remember, we are making that change when you take over Special Services."

"I remember," Lilly said, clearly irritated. The principals under the current organization chart reported to her.

Michael had conceded this to the principals, led by the three she-wolves, who had resented Lilly's orders and lack of respect toward them. They had met with DelVecchio when the reorganization was announced. Lilly also attended the meeting, and sat to DelVecchio's right.

"We will absolutely not stand for directives by some new guy from outside the district who knows nothing about Menlo Grove," stated Rosemary Grogan-Unangst, speaking for the group of five principals at the meeting.

Grogan-Unangst was attractive, personable, and politically astute, serving as president of the Menlo Grove town council, and major supporter of the current mayor, and she knew how far she could push Michael DelVecchio. He made certain Rosemary served on every important personnel committee. He knew that she possessed awareness of the political realities. He was smart enough to keep her close. The others at the meeting were smart enough to allow her to serve as their spokesperson.

Len Ferrigno attended the meeting and represented the four middle school principals. The serious-looking, burly man in his late thirties was on his way to a future superintendency. He dressed impeccably and would keep silent in front of the three elementary women principals, who were all present for this meeting.

The fifth principal at the meeting was Grace Romanczak, the smartest and most gifted educator of the group. She was tall and pencil thin, with a large curly mop of dark hair. Romanczak always wore a pants suit, and she always remained silent unless called on to speak. DelVecchio recognized her intelligence and talent. He called on her frequently for her opinions. She ran Henry Ford High School with precision. The high school she managed consistently rated as one of the top public high schools in New Jersey.

Lilly sat through the meeting holding her tongue. She would tell Michael her opinion immediately when the meeting ended. Not only did Lilly consider what the elementary principals did "not rocket science," she loved to remind them of her experience, beginning many of her directives at principal meetings with, "When I was a principal...."

The principals respected Lilly's knowledge, work ethic, and political savvy, but they hated her condescending tone.

Grogan-Unangst made a solid case for the principals to report directly to DelVecchio and not to the new guy. As the meeting concluded Michael told the principals, "Okay. I heard what you had to say. Let me think about it."

DelVecchio continued to the next topic. "We are having another building referendum for the public coming up in December to vote on funding renovations and additions to many of your buildings. Grace, what do you think?"

"The last six referendums have all been defeated," Romanczak said. "What are the chances this time? I desperately need more science labs so I can offer additional Advanced Placement courses. The parents in the North side of town are clamoring for more A.P. courses."

"So make sure they get out and vote in favor of the referendum," DelVecchio smugly stated.

"Trying to get my group of parents out to the polls is not so easy, Mr. DelVecchio," truthfully retorted Romanczak.

"I need all of you in this room to get your parents out to vote in favor of the referendum. We need to upgrade our facilities."

"Maybe if we hadn't given away so much in the teachers' contracts over the past twenty years, the district would have had more money to keep up our buildings," elementary principal and she-wolf Cyndi Zubricki flatly stated.

"None of us said that when we were teachers," DelVecchio replied honestly.

"Well, my building is falling down around me," Zubricki continued. "I have kids lining up in the hallways to get their lunch from a rolling cart and returning to their classrooms to eat. It's disgusting."

"Get your parents out to vote in favor of the referendum," DelVecchio repeated the mantra.

"I'll try," Zubricki responded glumly.

"We'll all try," stated the stolid middle school principal Len Ferrigno.

"Thank you," DelVecchio said, abruptly ending this meeting the way he ended all meetings.

After the five principals left the room, he turned to Lilly.

"What do you think?"

"It's going to be tough to pass that referendum in the current climate," she said.

"I know that. It's going to be next to impossible," DelVecchio admitted. "But we have to keep trying. Our buildings are a disgrace. I have sixty elementary students crammed into a lunch area, and we're calling it gym. The principals tell me some of the kids stand around waiting for a turn for most of the P.E. period. What kind of gym class is that?"

"Michael," Lilly said, "The number of times we've deferred maintenance on our buildings is disgraceful. Cyndi's right for once. We have buildings that are crumbling around us."

"That is why we need to keep offering these referendums," DelVecchio countered. "I am hoping eventually one will pass."

"Well, you can always hope," Lilly said.

"Okay, what else?" DelVecchio hated spending too much time on any one topic.

Why couldn't the principals just continue to report to me?" she asked.

"You will have plenty to do dealing with your new position and breaking in the new guy," DelVecchio replied. "Besides, you take care of the day to day that goes on here in central office and the Division of Student Services, and I will take care of the building principals."

He knew the principals and Lilly had an "agree to disagree" relationship with this issue.

"We'll touch base at the end of every day. You know that," he concluded.

DelVecchio decided that the principals, elementary, middle and high school, would report directly to him, as per the principals' own request. This afforded the principals more opportunities to undermine, complain, or ignore directives from the new Assistant Superintendent of Curriculum and Instruction, bypassing Lilly, as they now could not do. They would now not dare try to undermine, complain, or ignore Lilly, whom they knew DelVecchio held in total confidence and loyalty. They also knew Michael would hold no similar feelings or regards for the new guy.

DelVecchio conceded to the principals because he feared what they could do to his chances of being rehired. The state had eliminated tenure for superintendents, replacing tenure with three or five year contracts. The result allowed superintendents to become free agents, moving from one district to another as they negotiated higher and higher salaries a year before each contract expired.

The affluent districts drove this salary escalation, and the middle class districts strived to keep up. Superintendent salaries exceeding $200,000 were suddenly common-place. Without tenure, the new focus for superintendents was kow-towing to the Board of Education members who now had more power in micro-managing the district. Maintaining consistent educational leadership virtually disappeared.

Many of the principals in Menlo Grove were long-time district employees with tenure and therefore untouchable, but also highly respected in the neighborhoods where their school buildings were located. Budget votes and, espe-cially, Board elections, could be swayed by individual neigh-borhoods, or voting precincts, and DelVecchio needed the principals in his corner.

A Superintendent could be undermined by an outspo-ken or disloyal principal, who was much closer to the par-ents and the public than any Superintendent could hope to be. The principals wanted to report directly to DelVecchio rather than the new Assistant Superintendent, so DelVecchio would clear it with Lilly, grant the principals what they had proposed, and then announce that it was his idea.

Nearly everyone would be happy.

DelVecchio would tell this to the new guy. New guy Ferrone would begin his new job unaware of several impor-tant facts.

First, the principals would not report directly to him as they did when Lilly ran Curriculum and Instruction. Therefore, they were under no obligation to follow his directives regarding curriculum or instruction.

Next, the principals would not have to follow his recommendations when they sent potential teachers to his office for the district office interview.

Finally, they were aware that he might offer his opinions and insights of them to the Superintendent during their annual performance evaluation. However, principals knew that Lilly wrote those evaluations for DelVecchio.

This was not how Lilly had described the job to him, though he was replacing her. He would learn shortly that the arrangement had changed.

He had told the interview committee that he believed in collaborative leadership, because he saw this as the most effective management style for a twenty-first century model of public education.

Those on the committee, even though they hadn't experienced such a management style in Menlo Grove, believed the same. They also knew with Lilly still in the district, Ferrone would be powerless to move the district in that direction. They recommended him for the position anyway.

After meeting with DelVecchio, Lilly appeared happy with the arrangement. Having the principals report directly to the Acting Superintendent would keep control out of the hands of the new guy. Reporting directly to DelVecchio meant the principals would be reporting indirectly to her anyway.

The new guy would have to deal with it. What options did he have? He had already accepted the job.

THREE

THE NEW GUY

Michael Ferrone sat in the Menlo Grove administration building's waiting area outside the Board of Education meeting room. He was freezing despite the August temperature outside now approaching 90 degrees in the late afternoon.

"This central office building's thermostat must have been set on 60," he thought to himself. "I wonder what it cost to cool this place?"

He glanced one more time at his watch.

Hating the thought of ever being late for anything, Ferrone had arrived twenty minutes early for his 5:15 P.M. interview for the position of Assistant Superintendent of Curriculum and Instruction. He had driven directly from his current job, driving north on an updated state highway, then connecting to a much older, worn and pot-hole filled one, before entering the limited access freeway which connected the northern, heavily populated parts of the state with the Shore points.

After a short ride on the freeway and connecting to an interstate highway built some fifty years ago, he had exited on an old state highway heading north to the Menlo Grove administration building. Every major highway in New Jersey seemed to go through Menlo Grove: the freeway to the Shore, the turnpike connecting New York City and Philadelphia, a major interstate highway, as well as the numerous red light filled roads of the old state highway system.

No wonder so many people lived here; Menlo Grove, the fifth largest municipality in the state, was an easy commute to both New York City and Philadelphia. In addition, its train station allowed passengers direct routes to both Boston and Washington, D.C.

Ferrone again looked at his watch. The time was now 5:45. With the twenty-minute head start, he had been waiting fifty minutes and still hadn't seen a single person. No one at the front door, no one to greet him, no one to check to see if he had even shown up.

He got up and looked into the small side window of the door leading to the employees' only section of the building. Nobody in sight although the reserved parking spots in front of the building were filled with several high-end late model cars. He looked again through the large glass walls into the BOE meeting room. Empty. He sat back down.

The walls around him were filled with photographs of district high school graduates who had achieved some athletic, artistic, or musical recognition. In addition, there were some photos of championship football and baseball teams. He got up and looked more closely at these.

The football photos were old – from the late 1970s and early 1980s. They were the oldest photos on the walls. He read the names of the coaches. He spotted Michael DelVecchio's name as an assistant coach in 1978 and head coach in 1982. Ferrone recognized the name, as DelVecchio was the person to whom he had addressed his resume when applying for the position.

He was not surprised that the current Acting Superintendent was a former coach. So many administrators with whom Ferrone had worked throughout his thirty-three year career had been former coaches. Some made good administrators - some not so much.

Coaches generally possessed good managerial skills. One of Ferrone's former coaching colleagues used to say, "Good coaches, by definition, have to be good teachers."

The problem Ferrone had with the coaches turned educational administrators was they usually did not have much knowledge of curriculum or the delivery of instruction.

Ferrone was a former long-time coach himself – many years as a football assistant coach, even more years coaching baseball, include fifteen as head coach. He had even coached basketball for a few years. During the years early in his career he had coached all three seasons, leaving home in the morning before his two preschool aged children were awake. Some nights each week he would return home after practice and graduate school classes, and the kids were already in bed for the night.

He hated those days when he did not see them, but felt at the time getting the Masters degree was important to the financial future of his family. Every fifteen credits meant more money in his paycheck. Each degree meant another raise. So if he didn't see his kids every single day, it was the price he was willing to pay.

Coaching was what Ferrone liked to call the "second shift." The pay wasn't much, but it was additional income at a time when it was much needed to meet family expenses. Ferrone couldn't say he was unhappy when the coaching days ended. He had coached high school sports for so long – twenty-six years - it almost became as difficult to leave as an abusive relationship. Not only the long days, the interminable bus rides, but the constant abuse and second guessing from parents had gotten worse through the years. At some point one forgets that one can simply walk away.

Some aspects of the job had evolved for the better, however, during his coaching career. He recalled how, when he was twenty-four years old, he became an assistant to a newly hired head football coach, just twenty-six years old himself. The new head coach had driven his very young football staff to Boston for a coaching clinic.

The Board of Education, so desperate to return the local high school to its aged, winning tradition from decades past, had agreed to send the entire staff on the excursion, including giving the new head coach cash up front to pay for the jaunt. Indeed, new rules prohibited such prepayment today, but not back in the 1970s.

The new head coach checked his coaching staff into the hotel in the suburb of Newton, and declared, "Let's go; we're taking a road trip."

A short ride from the suburbs to Boston, and they parked the young head coach's green van in a fenced and barbed wired parking lot.

"Boys," the young coach announced. "Welcome to the *Combat Zone*."

Ferrone had read about his place, a failed experiment in legalized prostitution, triple X movie theatres, totally nude strip clubs in a four-block area of Boston. A newsweekly at the time had described it as an area of violence, including a recent murder of a Harvard football player, a strangling of a dancer, and gun trafficking.

"Looks like a war zone," Ferrone thought as the group walked across a garbage-strewn street. "We could be killed," he said quietly to one of his fellow assistant coaches.

"Hey, winning football programs come at a cost," the other coach replied with a grin.

At the first bar they entered, the skinny dancers strutted on a narrow runway, the new head coach held a fistful of cash in his raised hand. "Drinks are on the Board of Ed.," he shouted above the pounding music to his young staff.

Another of the assistant coaches, the irrepressible and irresponsible Gary Geiger, stood up and shouted to the thin blond dancing nude atop the bar, "I love you."

The high school football team won two games that season.

The young head coach soon left education to sell life insurance. The majority of the staff, however, stayed on and grew together.

One of the assistant coaches became the next head coach, and trips to strip clubs ceased. Every activity became a family affair.

"Picnic at my house," the new coach would announce. "Bring the kids."

"Does that mean we have to bring our wives, too?" Gary Geiger asked.

The irrepressible and irresponsible Geiger was known to the rest of the staff as "the man of no moderation." He had also stayed with the staff through the head coaching change. A couple of seasons later, a coaching clinic and trip to the East Coast's new gambling Mecca (no upfront cash from the Board of Ed. this time) meant dinners at low cost restaurants or diners. Everyone fully clothed.

The coaches stayed two or three in a local cut-rate hotel. Ferrone and Geiger shared a room. One afternoon, after listening to three hours of lectures on the twin veer offense, Ferrone entered the room to find Geiger hanging up the phone.

"You have to leave right now," Geiger announced.

"Why? What are you talking about?"

"I got a hooker coming up here," Geiger said. "Right now."

"Get the hell out of here," Ferrone answered. "No way."

"Look out the window."

Ferrone ran to the window and looked down from the fifth floor. A scrawny looking brunette was walking away from a phone booth on the corner of the block straight toward the hotel. Ferrone watched incredulously as she entered the front door into the lobby.

"You're crazy," said Ferrone as he sprinted out of the room down the hallway to the sanctity of the other coaches' room.

Twenty minutes later, the phone rang, and Ferrone picked it up.

"She's gone," Geiger said solemnly through the receiver.

Ferrone returned to his room to find Geiger slumped in a chair near the window. He looked glumly at the floor. "I don't deserve my wife and kids," he said to his shoes.

"What happened?" Ferrone asked.

"We did it," Geiger said slowly.

"You're an idiot," Ferrone responded. "I thought you had no money."

"I had enough."

"I cannot believe how stupid you are," Ferrone said bluntly.

"Not as stupid as you might think," Geiger rebutted.

Ferrone looked at him quizzically, "What do you mean?"

Geiger glanced up at his fellow coach with a smile. "We did it on your bed."

Ferrone confirmed at that moment that every day we decide just what kind of person we want to be.

As exhausting as life was back then, the arrangement seemed to work. Right now, as Ferrone continued to wait in the frigid waiting area of the central administration building, the coaching stories and young children all seemed like a lifetime ago.

A female face interrupted Ferrone's reflections.

"Are you Michael Ferrone?" the woman asked.

"I am," Ferrone smiled.

"The committee is running a bit behind," the middle aged woman wearing too much eye shadow offered. "They will be with you shortly."

"No problem," Michael said. "I'm fine."

The woman disappeared through the door, and Ferrone shifted in his seat. He needed to go to the bathroom. He had been waiting an hour for his interview, and hoped this wasn't a clue as to the way the district ran its business.

As he continued to wait, he thought back to his early days as an English teacher. The many faces that came and went through the classroom door and the countless grade books and lesson plans he had filled out and written through the years. He had nurtured and developed his classroom skills. The Masters degree in Reading helped his skills in teaching literacy. High school teachers tended to assign reading, but could not and therefore did not teach reading. Most assumed their students, regardless of the content, already knew how to read and should somehow use their decoding skills to discover meaning. Most students, however, continued to struggle with material they could not grasp.

In some ways, however, schools had changed. During his first year as a teacher, he had been monitoring a first period study hall in the cafeteria. One hundred thirteen students were in the study hall. It took Ferrone nearly the entire 40-minute period just to take attendance, check absence slips for the previous day, and collect hall passes for those entering late.

One morning a short, wiry young man had entered the side door of the cafeteria, directly from the student parking lot. He had obviously not checked in to the main office first, and he was obviously late for school. This thin, swarthy looking student sat next to a pretty senior girl who had been holding her head up with her left hand as she tried to stay awake. He began whispering to her and then he kissed her.

Ferrone stood up and began to approach the young man. He spotted the football team's quarterback with his head down on the cafeteria table. The boy seemed to be sound asleep. As a young assistant coach, Ferrone wanted to make sure the young athlete had completed his homework. Ferrone also wanted information on the late kisser. He nudged the quarterback.

"Hey, wake up," Ferrone said.

"Huh, oh, sorry, Coach," said the pimply-faced QB. "Late night last night."

"Who is that student sitting next to the blond?" Ferrone inquired.

"Oh, Coach, that's no student. That's Mr. Miller. He teaches Science."

Ferrone was horrified. He had seen this guy kiss a student. Now what?

"Okay, thanks. I couldn't remember his name."

Shaken, Ferrone left the study hall at the bell, rushing to his teaching assignment. Three periods in a row of teaching grammar and Sir Gawain and the Green Knight before a twenty-two minute lunch break, and then he would have to say something to someone about the kissing teacher. Or maybe he shouldn't say anything. This was his first year. No tenure. No protection.

At lunch Ferrone spotted the assistant principal, a long-time veteran of public schools and former basketball coach and shop teacher. The assistant principal leaned on the wall of the cafeteria as the students gobbled lunch.

"Can I see you for a minute?" Ferrone asked.

"What's going on?" Everything fine, yes?" asked the V.P., eyes scanning over the student heads in the room as he spoke.

Ferrone explained what had occurred in study hall: the late arriving person he had wrongly thought was a student, the senior girl, and the kiss.

"And he kissed the student," Ferrone concluded.

"Is Miller still doing that?" The V.P. asked rhetorically. "Don't worry about it. I'll talk to him."

Ferrone walked away, regretting he had said anything. He had obviously over reacted.

Again Ferrone's daydreaming was cut short, as a thin woman about Ferrone's age came bursting through the door leading from the BOE meeting room. Her hair was a curled, wild mass of salt and pepper, with streaks of blond. She was overdue for some coloring. She seemed to be in movement even though standing still.

Lilly Laboy stuck out her hand and spoke rapidly.

"I'm Lilly Laboy. You're Michael Ferrone? Happy to meet you. Thank you for coming in. The committee will see you now." She spoke in a rush of words.

Ferrone stood up, shook Lily's hand, tried to say something charming, but she had already turned her back to him and headed from whence she came. He followed her and they exited the large meeting room, which looked like the inside of a fish bowl, surrounded as it was with glass walls. She led him into a much smaller, darker room where a table of several interviewers sat and stared as Ferrone walked through the doorway.

He was about to meet the committee. And he had to pee.

FOUR

THE INTERVIEW COMMITTEE

Michael Ferrone entered the windowless room with four non-descript walls surrounding a dark, rectangular mahogany table. He held a legal pad in his left hand. The five members of the committee sat along one side of the table. Ferrone would sit opposite the committee members on the other side. Assistant Superintendent Lilly Laboy introduced Ferrone to each person, and each smiled gratuitously at him as he awkwardly shook each hand, made eye contact, and said as sincerely as he could, "Nice to meet you. Pleasure."

Each member of the committee had a folder containing Ferrone's resume. In addition, each had a scoring sheet, a rubric of several categories, and a pencil. Michael DelVecchio, Acting Superintendent and former human resources person, insisted that the scoring be completed in pencil.

Ferrone sat across the long table from the group, attempting to jot down either the name or position as best as he could remember about each person he had just met. He always carried a notepad and pen.

Sitting on the opposite side of the table to Ferrone's far left was Brenda Dredahl. She served as the district's testing coordinator. Since Menlo Grove was such a large district, with sixteen schools, organizing the testing materials sent by the state throughout the year was a major undertaking. Ferrone had been involved with state testing since it began almost twenty years ago. Checking in materials, counting and recounting, distributing throughout the buildings, training proctors, dealing with building principals and logistics. He hated it.

After the testing, as long as nothing major went awry and no irregularity report had to be completed and sent to the state, or God forbid, no test booklet had gone missing, materials then had to be recollected, recounted, packed, and returned to the state. Test results were returned to school districts from the state department many, many months later, analyzed by Dredahl, sent to individual buildings, and reported to the Board of Education.

As a former supervisor, Ferrone had become an expert in looking at test data and spinning the numbers into a positive report to the Board. Because English and Math had been the first two areas tested by the state, supervisors had long been expected to break down the numbers to use for curriculum development or to camouflage weaknesses to the BOE.

Lilly chose Dredahl for the committee for obvious reasons. She possessed more expertise on state testing than anyone else in the district. She alone understood the intricacies of disaggregated data, cohorts, clusters, and subgroups, as well the penalties imposed if a single building in the district failed to achieve benchmark scores for all of its groups. This included minorities, economically disadvantaged, and the big one: special education.

Because of No Child Left Behind, the federal law imposing standardized test benchmarks, special education students were expected to achieve success on state tests just like regular education students. Millions of dollars and larger and larger percentages of district budgets were being devoted to extra practice for the special education students so they could attain the mandated benchmarks. The special education students' continued failure to meet the benchmarks on the state tests proved the bane of any district with enough special education students to form what the state department of education referred to as a "sub-group."

A subgroup's failure to succeed in large enough numbers would cause an entire district to fall into the "Failing Schools" list. Some politicians loved to point to these numbers as proof that public schools didn't work.

"Tell us about your experience and opinions with state testing," Dredahl stated directly. "Specifically, your background in raising test scores."

Ferrone thought to himself, "I hope every question is this easy."

He began his response in an orderly manner. First, answering the question directly and succinctly. Next, offering an example to clarify what he had said. Finally, telling of a short personal experience to illustrate his example.

His response method had been developed through the years when he had gone on interviews and when he had conducted interviews as a supervisor. When asked a question: Be direct and answer the question in one sentence. Next, give an example. Finally, tell a story, and get out. Be direct, be honest, and keep smiling.

The questions from each member of the committee continued. The person sitting next to Dredahl was high school guidance supervisor, who looked as if this day had lasted about ten hours too long.

A long time district employee, and married to a retired fire captain in town, she was beneficiary of the generous contracts and retirements of the local public employees. Jill Hillebrand was hard-working, committed to her craft, and owned a sardonic sense of humor. Lilly had selected Hillebrand for the committee for her extensive experience in high school. She always gave an honest opinion and could see straight through a phony.

She smiled at Ferrone.

"What Advanced Placement initiatives have you developed to help college bound students?"

A former Advanced Placement Literature teacher, as well as a former district A.P. Coordinator, Ferrone had increased A.P. participation by large numbers in his last two jobs.

Answer. Example. Personal experience story.

When he finished answering, Hillebrand was still smiling. Easy.

Next to Hillebrand sat a middle school principal. Doug Durling had moved into the Menlo Grove district about fifteen years ago. Still, many in the district considered him an outsider. He had, in fact, replaced Lilly as principal of Lilly's former middle school when she had become Assistant Superintendent. Lilly always felt that Durling didn't measure up to her as a middle school principal, and she would share her opinion that the middle school had experienced a precipitous drop in effectiveness since her departure.

Still, DelVecchio had insisted on Lilly's making Durling part of the committee. A man, a rare commodity at the elementary and even middle school level, was needed on this committee. Also, DelVecchio had been impressed with Durling's ability to improve the morale at Lilly's former middle school. In addition, Durling had shown his loyalty to the district by constantly stating the positives of the Menlo Grove district, and never uttering a discouraging word. Loyalty was a top priority to DelVecchio.

Durling spoke softly, and his smile made Ferrone even more comfortable.

"What is your philosophy regarding middle schools, and how they fit into the K-12 structure?"

Durling was about 60 years old, but looked older. No one in the room knew that he would be dead before this school year concluded from the cancer forming inside him.

"Middle schools should be less like little high schools, and more like elementary schools," Ferrone stated clearly.

"Middle schools have evolved from bridges between elementary and high school, the original intent, into mini-high schools. This is a mistake," Ferrone said.

"For example," he continued. "High school teachers assign their students work, but often do a poor job of training student HOW to complete the work successfully."

He looked at each member of the committee. No high school teachers were present.

"Elementary teachers are masters at teaching HOW, not just WHAT."

He told a personal experience story of how, because he had a Masters degree in Reading, he had learned this from the many elementary teachers, almost all women, in his graduate classes.

As a high school English teacher, Ferrone had, in fact, tried to train students HOW to read the literature for mastery, and not just have students, those who had bothered or were able to read the assignment at all, to tell what the assigned story had been about.

He told a story of how he taught a strategy called "close reading" with both his Advanced Placement students and his at-risk students. Then he succinctly explained the technique.

This was a risky response, given the first committee member handled state testing and the other was a high school counselor. Ferrone felt he should have added some evidence of improved test scores and more students getting into the college of their choice.

"Better to talk too little than too much," he thought to himself as he concluded his response.

The two remaining committee members to the middle school principal's left smiled broadly at Ferrone's answer.

"Bingo," Ferrone thought. The two women, both elementary principals, really liked his answer.

The first was an attractive middle-aged woman, obviously of Irish descent, with two hyphenated last names. She was a former elementary teacher, content specialist, and current elementary principal, so she obviously appreciated Ferrone's recognition of elementary school's nurturing and training of the "how to" model.

Her name was Rosemary Grogan-Unangst, and her place on the committee was a given. Rosemary seemed to be selected for every committee. Evenings she served on the Menlo Grove Town Council. Served as president, in fact. Her direct connection to the mayor's office proved a vital link to Acting Superintendent DelVecchio. No one seemed to think any conflict of interest existed.

She continued to smile at Ferrone as he waited for her question about the importance of individual principal and building autonomy.

The remaining member of the committee was Anne Carillo, a dark complexioned woman, perhaps of Italian background. She had taught in middle schools in Menlo Grove, but now she served as an elementary principal. From the smile on her face she also like Ferrone's answer about the lost relationship between elementary and middle schools.

Carrillo's father had been a long-time district employee and former principal, now retired. He and DelVecchio had coached football together thirty years ago. The daughter proved herself a cracker-jack middle school teacher and just as good a principal, though now at the elementary level. She had never married and she missed the daily middle school drama. Tired of wiping runny noses and helping the little ones put on their boots so they would not miss the bus home, she hoped someday to return to middle school.

Carillo asked, "How would you describe your leadership style?"

"I believe in collaborative leadership. For example, before making a decision regarding curriculum I would listen to different stakeholders with expertise in that area. During my time in my past district, I talked to classroom teachers to find out what class they preferred to teach and why. I always told them I could not guarantee that I could give them everything they wanted, but that I would try. At that point each of the teachers would say to me, 'That's okay. I'm just happy someone finally asked.'"

Lilly shifted uncomfortably in her seat at the head of the conference table. The two elementary principals, meanwhile, had also taken notice of Ferrone's background in Reading and both asked similar follow up questions about reading instruction. Ferrone himself could not have better scripted the round of questioning.

Lilly Laboy had seated herself at the head of the conference table, listening intently and taking notes. She never

45

looked up as the questions were asked. She was about to ask the final question.

Lilly began, "Menlo Grove has a unique problem. Some of its schools have a very positive image, but some have a more negative image. What ideas do you have to bring together our district which has such a wide discrepancy of socio-economic backgrounds?"

By previously checking both the district web site and the State Report Card, Ferrone knew of Menlo Grove's two Americas. The South side of town had been originally populated by the unionized factory workers in the post World War II era. Many had worked in the large auto plant as members of the autoworkers' union, before the plant had closed forever fifteen years ago. Industry and factories had once filled the South side, and now most were closed, either sitting empty or razed and morphed into strip malls of pizza joints, nail salons, and custom frame shops.

The tests scores of the South side schools looked problematic. The federal No Child Left Behind law had placed some of these schools, despite the overall high standing of the entire school district, on SINI lists – Schools in Need of Improvement.

The North side of town, however, had been developed later, as the population had spread. More professionals, - doctors, lawyers, bankers – had moved into large, newly built split and bi-level homes on the North side during the time many of the Baby Boom generation filled the schools.

The newly arrived immigrants had begun to arrive beginning in the 1980s and became the new white collar professionals. Many of its students spoke another language at home. The town's mayor was of Asian descent, much to the chagrin of the old working class in the South part of town.

The test scores of the North's elementary schools, the two North side middle schools, and Henry Ford High School were remarkably high. Ferrone had been amazed when he checked the Math scores from some of these buildings. Dozens of students had gotten perfect scores in Math! Incredible. The Language Arts Literacy scores all showed far above the average of other school districts in the same socio-economic category.

Ferrone answered Laboy's question using the experience he had gained both from his current district, which had six high schools in six different municipalities, and from his long experience in rural county in the northwestern part of the state, where he had spent the first thirty years of his career.

Answer. Example. Personal experience story. Smile confidently.

Lilly Laboy offered no discernable reaction to Ferrone's response. She finished writing her notes, and stood up. Ferrone followed her lead.

He thanked everyone for seeing him, and Lilly escorted Michael Ferrone out the same way he had entered, and quickly told him they'd be in touch. He was anxious to leave, but waited by the door until Laboy returned to the committee. She seemed to be in a constant hurry.

Then he virtually ran to the rest room.

FIVE

THE ACTING SUPERINTENDENT

The second round of interviews for Ferrone consisted of writing responses to two questions, each based on a scenario about some problem confronted by a public educator. Ferrone quickly completed his responses. His years teaching high school students how to construct an essay response made his answers both organized and concise.

The first question asked how one would deal with an irate parent who charged the district with racial discrimination based on the fact that her child did not achieve a passing score on state tests, despite her child's high report card grades.

The second question revisited the scenario of unequal test scores in different buildings in a large district.

'This must be a very big issue here," Ferrone said to himself, recalling the similar question in the first interview.

The second round of questioners consisted of the four members of the Board of Education's Curriculum Committee. Lilly again met Ferrone in the waiting area. He had been waiting forty-five minutes past his appointment time.

Lilly introduced Ferrone to each Board member. She spoke far too quickly for him to remember or write down any of their names. They looked well into their 40s in age; one man seemed closer to 70.

The committee consisted of Debbie Duhan, a cute blond with a terrific smile, but her skin looked like it had be intimately familiar with about thirty years of first and second-hand smoke; Carla Casella, a tired-looking high school Science teacher still wearing her teacher uniform of purple twin set and black slacks; Margie Steinmetz, a serious-looking, square, honest-faced woman whose demeanor went from stern to smiling when she made eye contact with Ferrone; and Larry Griffiths, an older man, grey-haired, dressed in tweed jacket and faded flannel shirt.

Lilly took her usual seat at the head of the table. Each Board member asked a pre-scripted question. Obviously the committee members had asked the same questions before. Ferrone answered each simply and clearly, smiling as his eyes moved from one Board member's face to another.

The Board members' questions were much more general than the first committee's had been. The syntax of most questions was somewhat awkward, making Ferrone believe they had been composed by the Board members themselves, and obvious from the lack of specificity that the writers knew far less about the nuts and bolts of either curriculum or instruction than the first committee.

Again, Lilly asked the final question. Another round of polite thank yous, and another night ride southbound to the Shore.

Three days later elementary supervisor Lucy Williams watched new guy Michael Ferrone walk confidently past her in his dark blue pinstriped suit. Even though Lucy and current Assistant Superintendent for Curriculum and Instruction Lilly Laboy had their differences, Lucy was unhappy to have Lilly leaving curriculum to be replaced by this new, unknown guy in a dark suit who knew nothing about elementary education.

Michael Ferrone, the new Assistant Superintendent of Curriculum and Instruction, would be officially taking over Lilly's position. Yet Lucy remained unconvinced how much Lilly would actually be letting go of curriculum. That remained to be seen.

Lilly Laboy, meanwhile, would move to the position of Assistant Superintendent of Student Services. No one in the district thought for a moment, however, that Lily actually would be relinquishing any power or authority by changing positions, especially to someone with no knowledge of the district's power structure like this new guy.

This was the primary reason no one within the district even bothered to apply for the job Ferrone had been offered. In fact, this move by Lilly would give her even wider power of the district's workings, as she could now control not only curriculum and instruction, but student services as well.

The change of position would allow Acting Superintendent Michael DelVecchio to keep Lilly Laboy close to what had become the most important aspect of any school district – keeping the district safe from the constant litigation due to special education issues – while allowing her to remain the silent power behind curriculum and instruction.

The new guy, being from outside the district, had no idea what he faced. He may have had plenty of background and experience in both curriculum and instruction, but Lilly, having been named by DelVecchio as head of the interview committee for her replacement, would make certain she would lead the committee to recommend someone she personally approved.

DelVecchio himself knew little and cared even less about curriculum, instruction, or student services. He lived as a political animal that had usurped his current position through political means. And he had the perfect partner in Lilly Laboy, who would now control all three vital elements of the school district: curriculum, instruction, and student services. DelVecchio would continue overseeing the budget and dealing with the political machinations necessary in a large suburban municipality.

This time Ferrone was greeted with a smile by the receptionist wearing too much make up as he entered the administration building for his meeting with the acting superintendent. He strode past a few people as he walked down the hallway, but stay focused on the door of the Acting Superintendent's office.

At the end of the hallway he sat down and found himself once more counting the minutes past his appointment time and shivering in the waiting area. "Geesh, they keep this building cold," he thought.

"Mr. DelVecchio will see you now," a secretary's blond head appeared from behind a closed door. She smiled gratuitously at Ferrone, as he sat in the area just outside the Board meeting room, - a "fish bowl" - where everyone passing by the glass walls could see a prospective candidate's discomfort.

Ferrone had been waiting only thirty-five minutes this time. They were getting better.

As he entered the large, well-appointed office, Ferrone was first surprised at the size and quality of the furnishings in the room. He had been in Superintendents' offices before, but never had seen anything as luxurious or as large as this. Dark cherry furniture, including desk and oversized office chair, sat along the far wall. In front of the desk sat two sturdy matching armchairs.

The two men awaiting Ferrone's entrance sat at a round table surrounded by four heavy chairs, closer to the doorway. The room was carpeted, and on the walls were photos of DelVecchio receiving various awards.

DelVecchio rose halfway out of his seat and stuck out a beefy hand. "Michael DelVecchio. Sit down."

Michael DelVecchio was a son of Menlo Grove. Born, raised, educated. High school athletic star. He had left town to attend college in the Midwest following high school graduation, but found his talents not suited in the bigger pool of fish in his new surroundings. He soon felt homesick for the place where every one knew his name and reputation.

After struggling through an injury-filled football season at college, he managed to make it through his first year, but determined during break between semesters that he would not return for his second year. He transferred back home to a state college, left his gridiron career behind, and immediately following graduation was hired by Menlo Grove as a phys. ed. teacher and coach.

He soon married a vivacious Math teacher, moved from assistant to head football coach, followed by positions of department chairperson, athletic director, assistant principal, and principal. He and his wife raised a fine family. All their children were successful in their own right.

When a somewhat older fellow coach who had followed a similar career path as DelVecchio was named Superintendent, DelVecchio was approached about moving to central office and becoming the Director of Human Resources. The job basically consisted of running ads, reviewing resumes, setting up interviews, checking on credentials, and recommending names to the Superintendent for hiring. The building principals or supervisors conducted the actual interviews. The P.E. teacher and coach turned building administrator took the job.

DelVecchio counted on his two secretaries to complete the bulk of the actual work in Human Resources. They kept him up to date on what they were working on, and reminded him when a state report on personnel was due. He was in the office at 8:00 AM and out by 4:00 PM. On especially sunny afternoons, he would slip out early for a round of golf with one or two fellow central office administrators.

His sudden and shocking move a few years later from Human Resources to Acting Superintendent was one that shook even the politically jaded Menlo Grove school district.

"Glad to meet you," Ferrone said. "Thank you for seeing me."

"This is Dan Maris, our business administrator," DelVecchio said, introducing the seated round man.

Ferrone stuck out his hand. Maris took it while sitting, smiled a hello, but remained silent.

Ferrone had originally thought that this would be the usual rubber stamp interview with the Superintendent following the first two interview rounds. However, DelVecchio held a sheet of paper in front of him with a list of what appeared to be phrases. He stared intently at the paper and grimaced.

"What is this about?" wondered Ferrone to himself.

DelVecchio cleared his throat and squinted a bit at the paper in front of him.

"Tell me what you know about each of the terms I am going to read to you. Keep it short."

DelVecchio began reading the words on the paper, one at a time, giving Ferrone time to respond.

"Manifest Determination."

"Cumulative Progress Indicator."

"Induction Program."

"Disaggregated data."

"Bloom's Taxonomy."

"Multiple Intelligences."

"Adequate Yearly Progress."

"Safe Harbor."

DelVecchio read slowly, obviously not familiar with the terms he was reading. Someone else must have written and given him this list. Fortunately, Ferrone knew each term from his years dealing with each of these elements of public education, either as a teacher, a test coordinator, or, especially, as a supervisor.

As a supervisor, he was part of the front line in the delivery of instruction. Because he was no longer in the trenches like the teachers, some considered supervisors just middle managers and expendable during times of downsizing. However, a supervisor was the one person who actually saw teachers teach on a regular basis, read their lesson plans, worked with them on curriculum development, facilitated department meetings, and conducted teacher training, often behind the closed door of an office and often individually.

Principals managed buildings. Most were only vaguely familiar with the state standards. Supervisors managed the teachers in those buildings, and because of state testing, were intimate with the state standards and therefore, the instruction of those standards.

New teachers frequently sat in the supervisor's office with tears streaming down their faces after a long day.

"The kids won't listen to me. I am up until midnight writing lesson plans and correcting papers, I have no life," they would cry. "Why did I think I wanted to be a teacher?"

The first year was always a nightmare. No one was prepared for the onslaught of preparation, multiple personalities, and administrative chicken-shit duties. Young teachers spent at least one late afternoon each week in a local bar drinking with other young teachers.

A supervisor also provided the only adult-supervision for reviewing teacher-made tests. This practice often caused cringing and head cramps for supervisors. The utter lack of creativity on most teacher-made assessments withered the brain.

When DelVecchio had completed reading the list of terms, and Ferrone had responded in an abbreviated version of his usual reply method, DelVecchio turned to Business Administrator Maris.

"Do you have any questions, Dan?" Asked the Acting Superintendent.

Maris smiled mischievously. "Do you play golf?"

Both men guffawed.

DelVecchio then got serious.

"We have a building referendum coming up. We need to upgrade our school facilities. You will be needed to help sell the need for this money. Your job goes beyond just curriculum and instruction," DelVecchio's voice had gotten lower.

"No problem," Ferrone easily said.

DelVecchio looked sternly and straight at Ferrone. "I have been successful in my career because I have put together winning teams," he began.

"I have put together championship football teams, championship administrative building teams, and I built a championship team here at central office. Menlo Grove has always been a top district in the state and will continue to be so. Do you think you are up to the challenge of joining my championship team?"

Ferrone smiled broadly but only briefly. He had heard and delivered many, many locker room speeches through his numerous years as a coach, and enjoyed the fact that DelVecchio used some of that still. He glanced briefly at Maris, and followed by directly staring into DelVecchio's eyes. Ferrone put on his game face.

"I am, Mr. DelVecchio," Ferrone answered strongly.

DelVecchio returned the stare. "Okay, then. Thank you. Congratulations."

It was the last time that DelVecchio would ever again look him straight in the eye.

SIX

THE MAYOR'S OFFICE

The phone rang in Mayor Kim's office.

"Superintendent DelVecchio just called again," the mayor's secretary said. "He wants to know why you are not returning his calls."

"ACTING Superintendent, you mean," the Mayor reminded her. "He is still working as 'Acting' until the REAL Superintendent's contract expires.

Kim was against the "firing" of the former Superintendent Claire Smith in the middle of her contract. The move would cost the taxpayers hundreds of thousands of property tax dollars to pay her to sit at home. Still, he understood that when a Board of Education turned over, as it might every April during School Board elections, such occurrences were known to happen.

He had stayed silent publicly on the issue. For his own survival as mayor, he had to keep the three big unions in town - the police, the fire, the teachers - happy. No one got elected or reelected in Menlo Grove without the support of the big three unions.

"Acting Superintendent DelVecchio would like you to meet with him. At his office," the secretary said.

"Well, fuck him," thought Kim. No way was Kim going to meet with an old broken down former football coach on the coach's turf. DelVecchio was in his late 60s and may have been a former football coach, but the guy was far from broken down. He still possessed a barrel-chest and rigid mien. He looked like he could go on forever, despite a two-pack a day cigarette habit and the stress of the job. His mother was still going strong at 93 years of age.

"Tell Acting Superintendent DelVecchio my schedule is filled," Kim politely replied to the secretary, and hung up the phone.

Kim knew he was playing with fire. His election was big news in the state. First Asian-American mayor in state history. In addition to bringing out the Asian voters, he also had to get at least some of the Asian-Indian population to vote. This was a real challenge, as both the first generation Chinese-Americans and the Asian-Indians preferred to stay out of the town's politics. Kim was not yet forty years old, and many said he had a very bright future in state-wide politics.

Most important, however, Kim had to compromise a bit and assure the three big unions that he would do their bidding at contract time. This was becoming a real challenge as the town's budget and dwindling revenues made expansion and promotions in all three public sectors impossible.

Town revenues from ratables had decreased $50 million in the past year alone. This year looked even worse as more and more manufacturers moved their businesses out of state or overseas. Increasing profits for shareholders was the name of that game. The corporations considered the destruction of local manufacturing base in town collateral damage.

More and more buildings in town sat empty, reminding all residents who drove along Route 6 every day of how their town was changing. The tax base was rapidly shrinking. Kim was proposing not replacing a half-dozen firefighters' positions due to retirements. With benefits it would save the town almost a million dollars. The firefighters' union was outraged. Kim knew the police and teachers would soon follow in their ire.

A challenge from a local Republican in the next election was not a concern for Kim. Menlo Grove still resembled an old, industrial union town, with voter registration of Democrats outnumbering Republicans by 6-1. However, even though he had graduated from the local high school, some still considered Kim as an outsider. A primary challenge from within the party was not out of the question.

During the last Board of Education election, two candidates who were supporters of Kim were elected, ousting two of the three incumbents running for reelection. The two new Board members were vocal in their disapproval of the firing of the school superintendent and the promotion of DelVecchio to Acting Superintendent until the fired Superintendent's contract ended at the end of the following June.

There existed plenty of support for that position in town, but the unions supported the three incumbents. However, only one of the three challengers won reelection. Something was changing.

One winning challenging was Larry Griffiths, a retired Ivy League college professor who wrote obscure books on education and thought himself an intellectual. DelVecchio had no time for anyone who thought himself an intellectual. The other newcomer to the Board who made no secret of her unfavorable opinion of DelVecchio was Suzee Semanski, a curvy adjunct at the community college. She was determined to undermine DelVecchio in any way she could.

DelVecchio was unhappy with the election results. He had spoken to Board of Education president Bill Burton immediately after the election results became official.

"Damn it, Bill, I need five votes to be named Superintendent when Claire's contract ends on June 30."

'You still have seven," Burton replied.

"Oh, no I don't. Remember, only Board members with no relatives employed by the Board can vote," DelVecchio reminded Burton.

Burton was well aware of this part of the state's administrative code regarding superintendent appointments. He also knew that two current Board members had family members working as teachers in the district, and were ineligible to vote for DelVecchio's appointment as full superintendent. Burton was just trying to calm DelVecchio.

But that meant there were only seven voting members. And code stated a superintendent needed a majority of the FULL Board, meaning he needed to keep all five remaining supporters in his corner.

DelVecchio knew he needed to keep all three incumbents in office in order for him to secure a new contract.

"Okay, you still have the five votes you need. You don't need the two new members."

"Too close for comfort," DelVecchio grumbled.

"What are you going to do with Semanski?" DelVecchio asked BOE president and local attorney Burton. It was the president's responsibility to place Board members on the committees on which they would serve. New Board member Suzee Semanski needed to be placed on at least one committee.

"She's a college instructor, Mike," said Bill. "She wants to serve on the Curriculum Committee."

"Yeah, right," answered DelVecchio. "Put her on Building and Grounds with Vito."

"Board of Education member Vito Viterelli was a local contractor who knew construction and how to play to the camera which recorded all Board meetings for the local cable access channel. He stood all of 5'4", thought of himself as a Mafioso made man. In truth he was a small time bully with a big mouth and a red face. No one took him too seriously. He fully needed the step-up built into his two-ton pick up, which he enjoyed parking in the handicapped spots during his daily visit to DelVecchio's office.

Adjunct Suzee became Vito's partner on Building and Grounds. She would not be heard from again until the next Board election.

DelVecchio's secretary relayed the message from the mayor's office.

"The Mayor can not meet with you today."

DelVecchio grimaced. "Kim will regret the way he treats me," the older man thought.

His secretary spoke again. "Barbara Jean is on the phone," she announced.

"Oh, shit," said DelVecchio. "Now what?"

Barbara Jean Cox, elementary principal and one of the three she-wolf principals, caused consternation with her phone calls. Another elementary principal, Rosemary Grogan-Unangst, made calls that got immediate attention from both the Mayor and the Acting Superintendent.

Grogan-Unangst, another one of the three she-wolves, served as another card Mayor Kim had to play. She was the president of the town council, who happened also to serve as an elementary school principal in town. Rosemary Grogan-Unangst came to politics only after her fiftieth birthday, attracted by Kim's promise to change the old boy Menlo Park way.

She had been persuaded by her daughters to run for elective office and because she got support by the teacher, police, and firefighters' unions, she had won. Talented, smart, and charming, she had won reelection and elected president by the other council members.

Both Mayor Kim and Acting Superintendent DelVecchio had to keep Rosemary close. Kim would ask Rosemary what was going on in the school district, and DelVecchio would inquire of her what was going on with the town council. He also allowed Rosemary to serve on every committee on which she wished. She had DelVecchio's personal cell phone number, and if she didn't call him daily, he would call her. Grogan-Unangst possessed the savvy and ability to keep the two men both at a distance and in her control.

Concern about the mayor and the new Board members would have to wait for a while. Barbara Jean Cox was on the phone. DelVecchio picked up the phone delicately, knowing Barbara Jean was not calling to wish him a nice day. He was right.

"I don't want that fucking idiot in my building," she screamed into the receiver.

SEVEN

THE UNION BOSS

Principal Barbara Jean Cox was just completing the early morning walk through her building's hallways, making sure every classroom had begun the day's routines and hustling late arrivals to their appropriate rooms. She spotted Union President, Kristoff Kaifes, standing outside the doorway of one classroom. He was in soft conversation with a middle-aged third grade teacher.

Cox drew herself up to her full 5'2" height and walked directly up to Kaifes and stood less than two feet away from the two people conversing. Cox may have been small in stature, but she had always possessed other, bigger qualities. In junior high she was voted "Biggest Big Mouth," by her classmates, but the class advisor vetoed the original label, replacing it with "Biggest Gossip." Ironically, by B.J.'s senior year in high school her classmates voted her "Best Mouth."

Cox stared impatiently at the teacher. "Your students are in your classroom and they are unsupervised. I very strongly recommend you have this meeting on your time, not your students' time."

She turned and faced Union Boss Kaifes.

"Kristoff, I didn't know you were planning on visiting my building this morning."

"Good morning, B.J, I mean, Billie Jean," Kaifes said, grinning slyly while leering at the principal. Then he turned back to the teacher, "I'll be in touch."

The teacher quickly disappeared back into her classroom.

Kaifes enjoyed greeting women with a hug and a kiss, but those who had been in the district knew him well enough to keep their distance. Kaifes had recently celebrated his sixtieth birthday, though at that age in education, celebrate was probably the wrong way to describe another birthday as he was one of the dinosaurs. He served as association president in the district, a euphemism for union boss.

The position was full-time in a large district like Menlo Grove. Kaifes no longer had to teach class, had a private office with his own secretary, and the position paid $125,000.

For all the headaches of the job, and there were plenty, Kaifes knew it was far better than having to teach. He had gone into education because both of his parents had been teachers. He had been an excellent athlete in school, gotten a partial scholarship to play football in college, and his time as a student-athlete had been his best days.

In college he had trouble with some of his content-heavy classes, so he decided to become an elementary school major, hearing that was the easier path. Those classes were full of females, many of whom were more than willing to help the burly football player with the sly smile and full shock of dark curly hair with his class work and projects.

Following graduation, Kaifes had no trouble securing a job as an elementary teacher. Finding a man, especially a physically imposing man, in an elementary building was rare. Even if he wasn't the strongest of teachers, there were always women willing to lend him a helping hand.

One kindergarten teacher, in her second year of teaching, got her hooks into him almost immediately. They were married during spring break of his first year. Kaifes felt being married should have not undue influence on his nights at the bar or comforting other young female teachers. The kindergarten teacher soon realized her error in judgment and the marriage ended soon after it had begun. She found a similar job and much better husband in a neighboring district.

Unmarried male teachers did not stay single long. Besides being in the minority of virtually every school building, overwhelmingly so at the elementary level, male teachers generally were good catches. They were educated, had secure jobs with great benefits, and were nurturers of children by nature. Indeed, when women spoke in hushed tones about any male teacher's "package," they were not talking dirty about the man's private parts, but that he possessed not only medical, but both dental and vision insurance as well.

After his divorce, Kaifes soon rebounded, marrying a teacher in another building in the district. Together he and his second wife were married for twenty years and raised two daughters. Kaifes, through his affiliation with the local Knights of Columbus, had somehow gotten the first marriage annulled. When the second marriage also ended in divorce, he did not further pursue the Church option.

He was now on marriage number three. His current wife was not a teacher. Through his many years in the district Kaifes had managed both to work his way into the power structure of the union, and alienate nearly every female, whether teacher or administrator.

He was known as "the sleaze," and it was a name well deserved. The many years hanging out at bars after work had taken his dignity. Those years had also stolen his athleticism and physique. When women saw him walking in their direction in a school building, they generally headed in the opposite direction. If they didn't see him coming, they generally felt him as he always seemed to have to slide his way past them in the hallway, managing to move his hand over their hips as he passed. A workplace hug from Kaifes frequently was closer and longer than appropriate, as he always grazed for boobs.

Kaifes had developed a certain creep appeal that made most women teachers' skin crawl. Commenting on a new blouse or a tight skirt gave Kaifes an excuse to make compliments only he considered charming. Those receiving the comments either rolled their eyes or shivered silently in disgust.

Teaching was an intimate profession, and only teachers knew the demands of a job which included being locked in a room with two dozen children or adolescents for six or seven hours every day. After school intimacy and drinking with teaching colleagues often proved a combustible combination.

If one entered a bar late-afternoon on a Friday anywhere in the state, one was sure to find at least half the patrons were teachers. If it were an afternoon on a Monday through Thursday, then half those present were teachers with a drinking problem or either having or about to have an affair with a co-worker.

Ending the school day in mid-afternoon allowed teachers to develop friendships with fellow teachers which sometimes became intimate and often wrecked marriages. Many of the veteran teachers and administrators had experienced many affairs of the heart or had colleagues who had cried their regrets on friendly shoulders. Alcohol often proved a helpful ally.

However, finishing a school day at that time of day also permitted teachers to take second jobs, some coached or attended graduate school, while there were those that stayed late to complete their school work and prepare for tomorrow. Many others rushed home to get their own children off the bus or pick them up from daycare.

Union boss Kaifes those negotiations who had preceded him had negotiated a teachers' contract with language second to none. Through the years language had been added so the current contract included twice per year longevity clauses. Longevity meant a teacher would get a raise at mid-year and at the beginning of each year simply by staying in the district. Tenured teachers got what was called a "tenure bonus."

After only ten years in the district a teacher could be at the top of the pay guide, if one kept taking graduate courses. A teacher in his or her early to mid-thirties could easily be making 90K. Nearly 15% of teachers in the district made over $100,000.

Another special and costly clause was the extra pay teachers could earn by staying after school and helping students. When proper paperwork was completed, this "extra help," now officially called "supplemental instruction," meant another $50 per hour could be earned not only after school, but also each the school day during the teacher's planning period. This was the period each day when the teacher did not teach, but was given time to check their mail and messages, make a phone call, complete paperwork, go to the bathroom, or just sit in the faculty room, close her eyes and rub her temples.

Some teachers never took the period off, but earned several hundred extra dollars each month by meeting one on one with a youngster having difficulty in class. No Child Left Behind, also known as NCLB, meant every child had to pass the state tests, even those with learning disabilities. This mandate increased the need for extra instruction.

Special education was rapidly bankrupting nearly every district in the state. The cost of additional instruction, para-professionals, individual aides, out of district placements, including special door-to-door transportation, was running in the millions. For Menlo Grove the cost of running the Student Services division, excluding salaries, was already costing $40 million, or 20% of the district's $200 million budget.

In addition, teachers were also paid at the hourly rate to revise curriculum, another state mandate. Most districts paid teachers to do this task, usually during the school day, on a per project basis, but in Menlo Grove the pay was hourly. Classroom teachers while revising curriculum were replaced by substitute teachers. The substitute was paid $100 a day to keep the students quiet with seatwork while the sub sat at the teacher's desk and read the latest Danielle Steele novel. Curriculum revision was a slow and costly process.

The teachers in Menlo Grove were grateful for the union's tough negotiators. The Board members were grateful for the teachers' support in local Board of Education elections. Kaifes would not let the teachers forget his work for their benefit. Most knew his actual impact on negotiations was limited, since the long-accepted process of adding lavish language began while Kaifes struggled as a classroom teacher. Still he roamed the hallways like an aging peacock, strut still intact, but feathers faded and limp.

B.J. Cox now confronted Kaifes in the hallway. "I told you never to enter my building without calling ahead," she said angrily.

'Relax, Barbara Jean," he answered calmly. "You have a teacher that has an issue with Lucy, the supervisor. The teacher needed to talk to me."

"Kristoff, none of my teachers need or want to talk to you," she virtually spat out the words. "Get out of my building right now."

"It is not your building, sweetheart," he responded with a sneer. "This is a district building."

He walked out the front door as she steamed alone in the hallway, surrounded by primary colored doors and student work hanging on the walls.

"Son of a bitch," she said to herself, as she walked briskly back to her office to call Acting Superintendent DelVecchio to complain about what had just occurred. She had to do make this call immediately, for at 10:00 A.M. she had to run out of her building for a secret meeting with a high school supervisor with whom she was currently sleeping.

EIGHT

THE PRINCIPALS

Acting Superintendent Michael DelVecchio took the phone call from Barbara Jean Cox, principal of one of Menlo Grove's ten elementary schools, and known by some as prime instigator of the three she-wolves. She had originally been a primary school teacher in the district, and then became one of the charter members of the building specialists group. After serving in that position for a few years, Barbara Jean became the elementary supervisor.

The building specialist position had been created to replace elementary school assistant principals in a cost-cutting move. The curriculum specialists would be paid on the teachers' salary guide, which would cost the district far less than an assistant principal. The teachers' union fully approved getting rid of the assistant principals, who had power of evaluation over teachers.

The curriculum specialists had no such power over the teachers because they were in the same bargaining unit. A conflict of interest precluded those in the same collective bargaining unit from evaluation. Since they would remain in the teachers' union, the union leadership also liked the idea of increasing its membership.

Barbara Jean Cox had been passed over when she first applied to become a principal in the district, when an affair with a much older administrator in the district became public knowledge.

After being passed over, Cox had left the Menlo Grove district to take a job as a vice principal in a neighboring district, but had returned to Menlo Grove after having earned administrative experience in the other district, and after her paramour, twenty years her senior, had retired.

She had returned to the Menlo Grove district as a building principal with a vengeance and an attitude. She used both her elementary expertise and powerful personality to overhaul the direction of the elementary school building to which she had been assigned.

"Hello, Barbara Jean, " Michael DelVecchio said politely into his office phone.

"I don't want that fucking idiot in my building. I have told you that before, Michael," screeched B.J.

"Which fucking idiot is that?" DelVecchio asked sarcastically. He was used to these daily blowups by Cox, whose large ego and lack of patience were well known.

"That fucking sleaze Kaifes," she screeched into the phone, referring to the President of the Teachers' Union. Cox knew her sleazes from her long history of expending so much of her own energy on men of questionable morality.

DelVecchio blinked at the decibel level coming through his cell phone.

"Okay, calm down, Barbara Jean, let me talk to Kaifes. I have a meeting with him this afternoon."

Cox banged down the phone. She wanted DelVecchio to feel her anger, and to fear it. Both were well aware of Cox's sterling reputation as an administrator. She had a powerful hold on the family neighborhood surrounding her school building. In order to carry that voting precinct, DelVecchio needed to appease Cox, clearly one of the leaders of the district's administrators.

In addition, Cox kept close contact with a current Board member with whom she had attended high school long ago in Menlo Grove. It was no secret that the Board member still felt a longing for B.J.

Cox had joined with Rosemary Grogan-Unangst and Cyndi Zubricki to form the triumvirate of she-wolves and to move the other elementary principals in their direction. The person trying to keep all the elementary buildings on the same curriculum track was Lucy Williams, named elementary supervisor after Cox had left the district. Cox had no time for Lucy's idealistic approach.

With Assistant Superintendent Lilly Laboy moving from Curriculum to Student Services, the path was now clear for the three principals to run rough shod over Lucy, the new guy in charge of curriculum, and the other elementary principals.

Cyndi Zubricki, meanwhile, had moved from elementary teacher to building specialist to elementary principal smoothly. Trim, smartly dressed, and intelligent enough to hold her tongue until the time was right, she possessed just the right amount of balance to keep Grogan-Unangst and Cox moving in the desired direction. Her affinity for prescription drugs also assisted her in maintaining balance.

The other seven elementary principals consisted of four men, three of whom were former high school teachers and coaches who were appointed principal because of their leadership and managerial skills. None even pretended to know anything about elementary curriculum.

The fourth male was Jimmy Bede, now entering his fiftieth year as an elementary principal in the district and eightieth year on earth. His utter refusal to consider retirement – "My wife won't let me," he would say," - meant his building was run by his secretary and his building specialist. Jimmy seldom spoke at principals' meetings, using most of his energy trying to stay awake. He could, however, recite by memory the seven local restaurants he and his wife of fifty-seven years patronized each of the seven days of the week.

The other three female elementary principals had been hired from outside the district, and at least one of the three she-wolves, usually Rosemary Grogan-Unangst, made certain she had been part of the interview committees when each new principal was hired.

These three principals, or the "outsiders", as they referred to themselves, knew which principals were calling the shots, and they knew their place and kept in it.

When newly hired Assistant Superintendent of Curriculum and Instruction, Michael Ferrone, called his first principals' meeting, the three she-wolves sat together right up front. Rosemary Grogan-Unangst had sat on the new guy's interview committee, but all three women wanted to size him up more closely. And they wanted to make sure they sat close enough so he could size them up as well.

DelVecchio made an early appearance at the meeting. He liked the face time with the principals, but getting into their buildings proved difficult for him. His appearance at Ferrone's meeting immediately changed the timing of each agenda item that Ferrone had planned.

"Good morning, everybody," DelVecchio began. "I am confident you will work well with Mr. Ferrone to keep Menlo Grove's high academic standards."

"As you may know, we have a building referendum coming up. I need all of you to make this a top priority whenever you have parents in your building."

With that, DelVecchio began a thirty-minute ramble covering the reasons for the needed renovations and additions, the lack of adequate state funding the district received annually, the difficulty of getting the newly-arrived residents of Menlo Grove to the voting booths, and finally, the difficulties of dealing with the unreasonable Board of Education members and the expiration of his own contract.

Ferrone thought to himself as DelVecchio continued to ramble on, "My first agenda is completely shot to hell."

DelVecchio declared to those in the large room, "For continued stability, of course, I need to convince the Board to offer me a new contract. Of course, this is not about me but about keeping Menlo Grove's high standards," he stated without blinking.

"Are we sending out information about the referendum to the parents?" Menlo Grove South High School principal Sam Applegate shouted out, breaking DelVecchio's filibuster.

"Yes." DelVecchio made a face at Applegate because of the interruption. "My office will be doing a mailing to sell the referendum to every parent."

Elementary principal Rosemary Grogan-Unangst raised her hand, waited for DelVecchio to recognize her, and added her voice, "Those mailings to the parents are so expensive. Couldn't we just send everyone an email and a text message?"

"Our system is not set up for big emails, and I'm not even sure what you mean by a 'text message,'" DelVecchio grinned disarmingly.

Some of the principals made a sour face at the admission at how far behind the district had fallen with regard to technology. Fifty-year veteran of principal meetings Jimmy Bede's eyes fluttered as he attempted to keep them open.

"Call me if you have any other questions," the Acting Superintendent said finally to end what had suddenly had the potential to become a Q & A. DelVecchio hated a

Q & A.

"Thank you." DelVecchio turned abruptly and disappeared through the door leading to his big office.

Ferrone continued to sit for a moment after DelVecchio had left the room. He had sat down out of respect when DelVecchio suddenly injected himself onto the agenda and began the thirty-minute monologue. Now Ferrone realized the roomful of principals was staring at him.

He wanted each of the principals to introduce themselves, but realized that this could take longer than anticipated when old Jimmy Bede with his jet-black hair dye gave his name and then began reciting that since this was Tuesday, he and his wife would be ordering the shrimp scampi special tonight at The Italian Factory.

"I would like to tell everyone how happy I am to be here in Menlo Grove, one of the truly outstanding school districts in the state," Ferrone began.

"My long career as a middle school and high school classroom teacher, and supervisor in several districts in the state has brought me to this place to replace Lilly Laboy."

The principals openly smirked and shifted in their seats. Barbara Jean put her hand over her mouth to stifle a snort.

"Replace Lilly Laboy? No one is going to replace Lilly," she thought.

Ferrone continued, "My first goal is to meet with each of you individually in your building to find out what you feel are the most urgent curricular needs. I want to know how I can make your work lives easier."

Immediately, the principals made a mental list, as educators do, of prioritized items. Some, who never attended a meeting without a notepad, began making a written list.

He continued, "From my conversations with supervisor Lucy Williams, I appreciate and know the wealth of knowledge from which I will be able to draw from her. I know some of you and she have had many years of working here in Menlo Grove together. I will be counting on Lucy to assist me in setting a path to continue Menlo Park 's excellence."

The three she-wolves quickly grimaced, frowned, and glanced at one another.

Ferrone's words cut their way through the plastic smiles on the three principals' faces.

"Lucy Williams setting a path? Not a chancel" each of the three thought to herself.

Cox, Grogan-Unangst, and Zubricki, all dressed in new outfits from Talbots, would stay after the meeting to talk to DelVecchio about what they had just heard from this new guy Ferrone and who they trilaterally decided to undermine immediately.

NINE

THE BOARD OF ED

The under-sized auditorium in the fifty-year-old high school looked worn and tired. The thin carpeting added over the tiled aisles some thirty years ago appeared to be nearly translucent through wear. The dim lighting in the room created shadows among the barely dozen citizens who sat sprinkled throughout waiting for the monthly public Board of Education's Monday meeting.

The clock along the back wall of the auditorium read 7:30 P.M.

In the first three rows of the auditorium sat the district's principals and supervisors. Attending Board meetings became a mandatory part of their monthly job descriptions during a past superintendency. The superintendent at that time found himself consistently outnumbered by hostile members of the community, and insisted the administrators attend as a show of support.

The nine members of the Board sat on the stage. At the center of the dais the Board President, Bill Burton reigned. He ran the meetings by moving the agenda and recognizing speakers.

On Burton's immediate left sat Vice President Vito Viterelli, then Acting Superintendent Michael DelVecchio, attorney Bob Butterfield, and Business Administrator Dan Maris. Next to Maris sat Assistant Superintendents Lilly Laboy and new guy Michael Ferrone.

This would be Ferrone's first official Board meeting at Menlo Grove. To Board President Burton's right sat the other seven members of the Board.

The number of people sitting on stage nearly exceeded the number of private citizens in the audience.

The meetings were taped by a district employee and shown regularly on local cable access television. The more exciting moments could be found on the internet.

Burton led the attendees in the Pledge of Allegiance before settling down to business. Most Board meetings served as public settings for rubber-stamping the employment of new teachers, custodians, and other staff members, approving promotions, or acknowledging retirees. Approving expenditures took the largest segment of public Board meeting time. That is, until the public segment of the meeting, when those in the audience had opportunity to ask questions.

"Mr. President," Board member Debbie Duhan raised her hand thirty minutes into the proceedings. "What is $300,000 that we are approving for extended school year transportation mean?"

"Doesn't matter," Board President Burton smirked, "we already just approved it."

A member in the audience groaned aloud.

Vice President Viterelli noticed the groan and turned to Burton. "I would also like to know what we just approved."

Burton looked at Acting Superintendent DelVecchio for an explanation of the expenditure. DelVecchio shrugged his shoulders and looked at Business Administrator Maris. Maris shrugged his shoulders and looked at Assistant Superintendent Laboy.

Laboy knew the answer. "This is what it is going to cost the district to pay for bussing for our extended school year students."

"Extended school year?" Viterelli asked.

DelVecchio whispered to him, "Summer school."

"We are paying the students who flunked their classes to get to summer school?" Viterelli asked rhetorically. "That didn't happen in my day when I flunked classes."

Two principals in the audience giggled softly. Board President Burton suppressed a smile.

Laboy continued, "Most of the students being transported are elementary students who qualify for the extended year due to a disability or very low reading scores. The extra summer instruction helps them get up to the level they need to be so they pass the state tests."

"Hopefully they pass the tests," Burton added.

Following the normal business of the evening, the public segment of the meeting began. Members of the audience were permitted to ask Board members questions at the podium and microphone set up in front of the stage.

From their perch on stage, Board members peered down at the public.

Three people straggled up to the podium. One stood behind the other forming an abbreviated queue.

First in place stood an older man wearing a flannel shirt and worn denims and an old nylon windbreaker. The man appeared bent over slightly at the waist.

Behind him in line was a forty-something woman in an old housedress and crazy hair. She had her arms folded in front of her chest as she slowly rocked from left to right.

The only person in line that Ferrone recognized was Union Boss Kristoff Kaifes, who stood behind the crazy-haired woman in line.

"State your name and address, please," Board President Burton directed to the first questioner.

"Steven Szygieski, 25 Ben Franklin Road, Menlo Grove," the old bent man in flannel said.

"Hello, Mr. Szygieski," Burton said. Szygieski never missed a monthly Board meeting, and always asked a question. He found this more entertaining than sitting home with his wife watching reality shows.

The old man began talking without acknowledging Burton. "I saw Mr. DelVecchio driving the other day, during work hours, mind you, along Oak Hill Avenue. Were you driving there, Mr. DelVecchio?"

"Direct your question to the President," Burton reminded Szygieski. "You know the rules."

"Was he?" the old man asked the question to Burton.

"Mr. Szygieski," Burton responded in a slow, measured tone, as if addressing a child. "The Superintendent, er, Acting Superintendent is called on every day to visit schools throughout town during the work day. It is part of his job."

Szygieski ignored the response. "Was he driving a blue SUV?"

"Yes," Burton responded. "Mr. DelVecchio drives a blue SUV."

"And does that SUV belong to Mr. DelVecchio?" the old man continued.

"The Board has supplied its superintendent with a vehicle for completing district business for a number of years, Mr. Szygieski," Burton impatiently replied.

"My tax dollars are paying for that vehicle and you are telling me it is school property. Is that right?" Szygieski continued like a trial attorney leading a witness.

"Mr. Szygieski," Burton said, "what is your point?'

"My point," Szygieski retorted, "is I don't think I should be paying for Mr. DelVecchio to drive around town in a vehicle which he also drives to the diner for lunch and home every day."

Szygieski continued, "But since there is a state law against smoking on school property, and you just said that the SUV is school property, then can you tell me why Mr. DelVecchio is allowed to smoke while he is in that vehicle?"

For once Burton sat speechless. He looked at DelVecchio, who sat staring blankly straight ahead. DelVecchio's smoking addiction was no secret. He never smoked in the central office. He took numerous smoking breaks every day by leaving the building, getting into the SUV, and driving away while lighting up his brand of choice since he began smoking as a fifteen year old.

Burton himself was a lawyer, but he looked past DelVecchio to the Board attorney, Bob Butterfield. Burton could see that Butterfield was not paying attention.

"Mr. Butterfield, tell Mr. Szygieski why it is not illegal for Mr. DelVecchio to smoke in the SUV."

Butterfield, upon hearing his name, immediately broke into attentive mode. "Do you have documented proof that there is smoking going on in the vehicle in question?" Butterfield easily turned the question back to the questioner.

"I saw him," the old man muttered softly.

"Okay," Board president Burton broke in, "you have asked your hypothetical question, but since you have no documented proof, we do not have the time to answer every hypothetical question. Thank you for coming tonight. See you next month."

The bent man in flannel stood confused for a moment at the podium, then turned around and returned to his seat.

The woman in the housedress and crazy hair stepped up to the microphone.

"Name and address, Ma'am," Burton repeated.

"Hazel Dryden, 93 Washington Terrace, Menlo Grove."

"Yes, Mrs. Dryden, what is your question?" Burton asked.

Immediately the woman began shouting. "I want to know why my child was embarrassed in public by a teacher at the last assembly."

No one on the stage knew what she was talking about.

"Mrs. Dryden," Burton began, "I do not know to what you are referring, and from the look on Mr. DelVecchio's face, I do not think he knows either. Do you, Mr. DelVecchio?"

DelVecchio stared stone-faced straight ahead.

"I'll tell you what I am talking about," the woman at the microphone continued. "You have teachers in this district who got no respect, and I want something done," the woman was screeching now.

Burton broke in. "This sounds like a personnel matter. Mrs. Dryden, the law forbids us to discuss personnel in public. I will ask about your question when the Board goes into closed session."

Mrs. Dryden now turned her back to the Board members on stage and faced the many empty seats in the auditorium. She looked to the left of the video camera position against the rear wall of the room.

"You see, Harry," she shouted toward a gray-haired man sitting toward the back of the room. From the unconcerned look on his face, the man named Harry must have been her husband and must have heard the tone coming from her mouth many times before.

"These people won't talk to us," she shouted to Harry.

"Mrs. Dryden," Burton tried to calm her. "We cannot discuss a personnel matter in public."

The shouting woman turned slowly back toward Burton. "Well then, I'm going home to watch the Jets on Monday Night Football. She moved up the aisle toward her husband. "Let's go, Harry." And raising both of her arms above her head, she yelled, "Touchdown!"

She walked past where Harry was sitting, and the man slowly got up out of his seat and followed her through the exit door at the rear of the auditorium. A security guard followed them to the front door of the building.

The Board members and the administrators in the audience looked at one another in wide-eyed, stunned silence.

Union Boss Kristoff Kaifes stepped up to the microphone.

"Mr. Kaifes, how are you tonight?" Burton said almost in relief, as the Union Boss approached the podium and microphone.

When Kaifes began speaking, the women principals in the audience shifted uneasily in the uncomfortable seats.

Kaifes

A few rolled their eyes at one another. One made a face like she had just bitten into a rancid lemon.

"Kristoff Kaifes, 36 Monroe Street, Menlo Grove, and president of the Menlo Grove Teachers' Association."

Kaifes made a monthly pronouncement to the Board, and especially to the camera and his union members who bothered to watch from home. In fact, very few did.

"I would like to take this opportunity," Kaifes began, "to thank the members of the Board who continue to support the many gifted and hard working teachers of this great and proud district."

"Anything else?" Burton asked, his patience short and energy exhausted.

"And I would like to again express my appreciation," Kaifes continued, "to thank those teachers who are home tonight grading papers, making lesson plans, and preparing for tomorrow's school day."

"Thank you, Mr. Kaifes. The members of the Board thank the teachers as well," Burton added.

Burton scanned the audience.

"Seeing no one else with a question, motion to adjourn? Second? Mr. Maris, please read the statement."

Dan Maris, Business Administrator and Board Secretary, read aloud a statement explaining the purpose of the closed session, which would be commencing as soon as the auditorium cleared.

The remaining audience members, the principals and supervisors, and the Board members stood and stretched. A number of people, including Ferrone, headed for a rest room. The clock read 9:22 P.M. Ferrone had put on the suit he was wearing nearly sixteen hours earlier.

Acting Superintendent Michael DelVecchio and Board member Debbie Duhan walked directly to the exit door at the back of the stage so they could go outside and stand behind the building for a smoke while waiting for the closed session meeting to begin.

PART 2

SECOND MARKING PERIOD

TEN

THE SUPERVISOR

When Lucy Williams, elementary supervisor, checked her work mailbox in the central office building early one morning, she found a large manila, inter-office envelope signed by Acting Superintendent DelVecchio's secretary. Inside she found a resume with a note attached. The note read, "Interview this person." DelVecchio had initialed the note.

Lucy rolled her eyes. She had become used to conducting courtesy interviews. These requests occurred with nearly every teacher opening. A handwritten note to conduct a courtesy interview came when someone connected politically or having a personal relationship with someone in upper administration made the request.

Sometimes the resume belonged to a relative of the administrator or a Board member, but just as often came from a neighbor or from someone connected to the police or fire union.

Most of the time the courtesy interview was conducted and that was that. However, sometimes the courtesy person was hired over the supervisor's own recommendation. In those instances, the H.R. director would request the top two candidates be sent to him. Of course, one of the candidates had to be the courtesy interviewee.

Lucy checked her calendar and looked for an open hour to schedule the interview. After the secretary to the team of ten supervisors had been cut for budget reasons, the supervisors assumed responsibility for setting up their own interviews.

The secretary in Human Resources completed the initial screening of resumes, checking that the candidate possessed proper certification to teach. Nearly half of the resumes sent to the central office came from people without proper certification. Sometimes an unqualified person fell through the cracks and the resume got through to the supervisor.

Lucy remembered once reading a cover letter that began, "Hello, I am a retired Marine corporal, and am interested in spending my retirement as a fifth grade history teacher."

The cover letter came from someone who had no qualifications to teach. His interest in spending retirement as a teacher proved even too absurd to upset Lucy. Indeed, sharing the most ridiculous and outrageous cover letters and resumes became a regular late Friday afternoon practice for the supervisors. From the sublime to the ridiculous.

An hour after arriving at work, Lucy headed out of the central office for the parking lot. Her goal this morning included observing two elementary teachers conduct Science lessons. The drive through the neighborhoods in Menlo Grove proved time consuming as traffic crawled through the heavily trafficked streets during the day. Lucy's daily drive to the different elementary schools proved both challenging and time-gobbling.

"Take out your homework. Who does not have their homework?" The teacher shrieked at the ten year old students in the room.

As the lesson progressed, Lucy frantically looked through the Core Content Standards trying to discover what standard the teacher was addressing. No objective appeared on the board, and the teacher had not explained her goal to the students, so Lucy scrambled through the list of curriculum standards she kept with her for occasions such as this.

Since the state began testing, first in Language Arts and Math, then in Science, Lucy emphasized the necessity of constructing standards-based lessons. Many teachers who began their careers before curriculum standards existed believed they knew what the students needed more than the master teachers, supervisors, and directors the state had gathered to develop the state standards.

Even with close supervision, many teachers tried to continue to teach the way they always had. Without close supervision, Lucy couldn't even imagine just how disconnected instruction would become.

As Lucy walked through the hallway following the lesson, a new teacher hired the previous year per Lucy's recommendation approached her.

"Hello, Mrs. Williams," the young teacher said.

"Hello, Melissa. Please call me Lucy."

"May I talk to you in private? I have library duty in five minutes, so I am in a big hurry," said the teacher.

Lucy escorted the woman into a small supply closet and kept the door open.

The young teacher looked nervous.

"What is it, Melissa?" Lucy asked her.

"I don't want to get anyone in trouble, but my special education partner told me yesterday that she helped two of her students on the last state test."

Lucy remained calm. "What do you think she meant by 'helped'?"

"She said she told them to eliminate two of the obvious wrong answers on the multiple choice. She showed them the two obvious distracter choices, and then directed the students to choose between the remaining two responses." The young teacher seemed to gain confidence as she spoke.

"I appreciate your telling me," Lucy said. "I will take care of it."

"Thank you. I don't want to get anyone into trouble, but it doesn't seem right that some students get such help."

"You're absolutely right," Lucy replied. "You have done the right thing. I appreciate it. Thank you so much. Don't worry. I will take care of it, and you will remain anonymous."

"Thank you so much, Mrs. Williams. I feel so much better. I couldn't sleep at all last night."

The young teacher headed for the library leaving Lucy standing in the supply closet. Lucy's shoulders drooped, and her feet began to hurt.

Before leaving the building, Lucy stopped at the main office to check in with the principal, Scott Perrillo. Perrillo had been moved from a vice principal's position at Menlo Grove South High School to become an elementary principal. The only background in elementary Perrillo possessed was when he attended elementary school as a student some thirty years earlier.

The practice of placing a person with strong managerial skills, but not elementary experience, in the principal's chair of an elementary school was not unusual. Menlo Grove did this to "break someone in" as a building principal, as if running an elementary school was just a warm up for running a building in the upper grades.

And, although high school people were frequently placed in elementary school administrative positions, seldom did an elementary person secure an administrative position in a high school. Nothing irked elementary people more, and Perrillo quickly recognized his shortcomings and acquiesced to the three she-wolf principals so as not to alienate himself further.

"Oh, hi, Lucy. Great to see you. Thanks for stopping by." Perrillo was truly happy to see Lucy as he relied on her expertise. He recognized his lack of knowledge in elementary education, but he was as game and honest as he was clueless.

"I saw Mrs. Dover this morning teach a Science class," Lucy said. Lucy liked Scott, but she knew the three she-wolves easily and regularly rolled him. He was a good leader and building manager, but their knowledge of elementary curriculum and instruction overwhelmed him, and he felt without ammunition to counter their arguments.

"Oh, great. Great. Good lesson, I hope," Perrillo offered.

"We'll talk," Lucy replied curtly. "And I need to talk to you about something else. Very important." Scott stopped, and looked at Lucy.

"But I've got to run right now. DelVecchio wants to see me about something. Talk soon, Scott."

"Okay, great. Call me," Perrillo answered as Lucy hurried out the door and returned to her car. She made a mental note that she would call Perrillo later about what Melissa had told her about the testing irregularity. Going to the Special Ed supervisor might prove troublesome, as the Special Ed person would go into a defensive mode. Lucy would talk to Scott instead. It happened in his building, after all.

After arriving back at the central office, Lucy walked into DelVecchio's reception area. His secretary told Lucy that he was waiting for her. Sitting next to DelVecchio at the round table were Board attorney Bob Butterfield and elementary principal Cyndi Zubricki, one of the three she-wolves.

"Lucy, do you remember the second grade teacher you did not recommend to rehire two years ago? The one with the limp?"

"Of course, Judy DeCalma," Lucy recalled the young teacher with the slight physical disability. Everyone hoped she would serve as an inspiration to the children. Judy DeCalma had overcome a disability and had achieved throughout high school, college, and received a glowing recommendation from her cooperating teacher during her student teaching experience. The only problems, Lucy found, was the young woman could not teach, and she did not take criticism well.

DeCalma had been assigned to Zubricki's building. The young teacher had taken an inordinate amount of time from both the supervisor and the principal. Despite some serious problems, the district had decided to keep DeCalma after her first year. She had shown enough grit, work ethic, and intelligence to earn a second year.

Supervisor Lucy and principal Zubricki had constructed a professional improvement plan for the young teacher for year two. Year two had gone no better. Lucy recommended not reemploying. Zubricki agreed. Judy DeCalma's contract was not renewed for year three.

"Well," DelVecchio continued, "we have been contacted by legal counsel representing DeCalma. Said we have violated the Americans With Disabilities Act. The district is being sued for discrimination."

Lucy looked wide-eyed at Cyndi. Cyndi sat with her usual sardonic smile. "That's ridiculous," Lucy said.

"It may be," Attorney Butterfield intervened, "but it's happened and you will be called and deposed next month."

"Deposed for what?" Lucy asked fearfully.

"For recommending the district fire someone because of her disability," Butterfield replied.

"Gather together all your observations and evaluations for her," DelVecchio said. "Organize anything you have written, including emails and dates and notes of meetings with her. Include the dates and agendas of all the training she received. Be sure to include the sign in sheets so we have proof she was present. Give everything to my secretary. Our counsel will review all the material, and then copies sent to DeCalma's attorneys. We need the material by the end of the week."

Lucy left DelVecchio's office in stunned silence and clearly shaken. She had wanted to do a second classroom observation and write up both this afternoon, but her plan for today was now suddenly and drastically altered.

She returned to her office. On her desk sat a newly arrived stack of lesson plans. The stack appeared about two feet in height. The new guy's demand to have the teachers send copies of their lesson plans electronically was being met with some resistance by about half the veteran teachers, who continued to send hard copies.

Lucy began to gather the materials about Judy DeCalma that DelVecchio had requested. About an hour later, Bobby Jones, the P.E. and Health supervisor, came bursting into Lucy's office.

"Get a look at this," Jones said.

Lucy looked at the photo Jones had just handed her. The photo had been sent to Jones via email from a parent. Jones had printed the photograph from his computer. The photo showed students in the classroom worked quietly on worksheets. The older teacher was sitting at his desk, clearly asleep.

Lucy's shoulders slumped again. In addition to her aching feet, now her head hurt, too.

Bobby Jones and Lucy Williams had known each other for a long time. They had both been hired as teachers more than thirty years ago. Jones was a lifelong resident and former championship coach at Menlo Grove. He stood as living proof that good coaches made good teachers and possessed the leadership to serve as effective supervisors as well.

"I got to get this guy to retire," Jones said to Lucy. "He is killing me. Killing me."

"Did you hear I am being deposed for firing a teacher because of her disability?" Lucy asked.

"No shit?" Jones replied. "Well, listen to this," his competitive nature demanded he meet her story with one of his own.

"I had to meet with DelVecchio and the lawyer this morning, and my wrestling coach is going to be fired."

"What did he do?" Lucy asked.

"The father of a cheerleader found the coach had texted her filthy messages about a party they had attended together."

Lucy did not seem to understand. "The coach partied with a cheerleader?" Being an elementary supervisor had kept Lucy free from such high school hijinks.

"Yeah," Jones reported. "Apparently after matches he partied with both his wrestlers and the cheerleaders at the home of one of the wrestling club boosters."

"Oh, my God," Lucy said. "Is he tenured?"

"Doesn't matter," replied Jones. "DelVecchio said either he resigns immediately or the district will contact the police and let them take over the investigation."

"Couldn't the union get him suspended with pay?" Lucy asked.

"They could, but luckily the coach's mom is a long time librarian at one of the middle schools, and the dad is a cop in town, so they prefer to keep it quiet. DelVecchio said if the coach resigns DelVecchio will make sure he gets a good recommendation letter. The coach will resign and luckily will find something somewhere else.

"Luckily," Lucy ironically repeated the word.

English supervisor Dina Thomas entered the already crowded room. "What's this, a supervisors' meeting?" Judy asked, seeming not as full of cheer as usual.

"No," Lucy answered. "We're just sharing stories."

"Well, listen to this. I just came from the new guy's office. He has gotten several calls from the same parent. Seems Leonia Calabrese, one of my English teachers, gave a high school student a zero for failing to submit a research paper by the deadline."

Dina loved telling these stories.

"Did Ms. Calabrese have the student and parent sign a pre-nupt?" Jones asked, using the slang term a supervisor invented for having teachers pre-empt the usual student excuses about not knowing the requirements of an assignment.

The supervisor had borrowed the term pre-nupt from a wealthy person's pre-marriage agreement about how much a failed marriage would cost. Many headaches could be avoided by having both the student and the parent sign ahead of time that the student would meet all the teacher's requirements.

"What did the new guy say?" Lucy asked.

"He backed me all the way. At first," Dina answered, "but then he said after getting no satisfaction with him, the parents had subsequently called DelVecchio and after the new guy had been called in for a talk to DelVecchio, the new guy called me in and asked if my Leonia wouldn't reconsider and at least grade the student for the work he had completed. She could mark it late and subtract some points, but couldn't give the kid a zero."

"Slow down. Take a breath. What about the teacher's deadline?" Jones asked Dina

Thomas.

"The deadline is dead," Dina replied.

"Will your Ms. Calabrese agree to grade it?" asked Lucy.

"Yes, I think she will, but I will have to spend a lot of time persuading her. And Leonia will tell all the other teachers in the teachers' room that I didn't back her, and at scheduling time in the spring I know she will remind me that I owe her big time."

"Sounds like Leonia won't be teaching last period of the day," Jones chuckled. High school teachers loved having their prep period last period of the day. This effectively ended their official workday at about 1:30.

"If I get off that easily, I'll consider myself lucky," Dina Thomas concluded.

Lucy's phone began ringing. The caller I.D. showed Libby Laboy's office number.

Lucy suddenly realized that her shoulders, her head, and her feet were killing her. "How many days until Friday?" she wondered aloud.

She looked up at the clock. 4:30 P.M. She decided to write the observation report at home. She called Scott Perrillo to tell him about what Melissa, the young teacher, who had shared with Lucy her concern about the special ed teacher helping students on the state test. The phone was not picked up. Lucy left a short message, too vague to inform Scott of much but with an urgency concerning a testing situation. The phrase "testing situation" always got a principal's attention.

Lucy's commute would take nearly an hour. She planned to stop at the grocery store close to home to pick up something for dinner. When she finally pulled into her darkened driveway, it was 6:20 P.M. She had left the house more than twelve hours ago. She entered the house to find her husband asleep on the recliner. Newspapers were strewn on the carpet.

She walked past him into the kitchen and began to prepare supper.

ELEVEN

THE ASSISTANT SUPERINTENDENT

When the phone rang in Lilly's office, it interrupted her rewriting of DelVecchio's statement regarding the upcoming building referendum. Menlo Grove, despite its enormous population growth over the past three decades, had not built a new school building in nearly forty years.

Six consecutive building referendums had been defeated. Number seven was scheduled for the Tuesday before the December holiday break, just ten days from now.

Buildings strained at the overcrowding, often caused not just by more new students from new places, but by the numerous mandated new programs. At the time these buildings were constructed, programs for special education, severely disabled, autism, English as a Second Language, even most sports programs for female students, didn't exist. Even so, most of the school buildings lacked space for cafeterias, auditoriums, or libraries.

Every open corner, cubby, or alcove was now used as part of "pull out" programs, where students were excused from their class to get individualized one-on-one instruction. This extra instruction was part of the classified student's Individualized Education Plan, or IEP, and since the IEP was a legal document, the very expensive practice of one-on-one instruction existed as a legal mandate.

"Maybe I have taken on too much," Lilly thought to herself as she rewrote DelVecchio's pedestrian words. He relied on Lilly not only to give him advice on academic decisions, but also to do handle much of his writing chores.

Everyone knew that Lilly, not DelVecchio, wrote the evaluations for each of the principals, and then she sent the reports to DelVecchio for his signature.

"What is it?" Lilly snapped into the phone as she answered it.

"Get down here now," DelVecchio growled at the other end of the phone. "We've got a problem."

Lilly immediately hung up the receiver, put down her editing pen, and headed out of her office and toward DelVecchio's.

DelVecchio sat behind his large desk, holding his head in his liver-spotted hands. He looked up at her. She found herself struck by how old and small he suddenly looked, the skin of his face pallid and dark circles surrounding his shrunken eyes.

"Three building and grounds workers have been arrested for robbing a bank on Elysian Avenue," DelVecchio began.

"What?" Lilly screamed.

"Okay, allegedly robbing a bank," he said.

"So fire them immediately," Lilly answered.

"Not that simple, Lilly. One of the guys arrested is Danny Wells."

"Oh, shit," Lilly said.

Danny Wells was the youngest son of Daniel Wells, member of the Menlo Grove Board of Education. Lilly already had plenty of unpleasant history with Daniel Wells. She had tried to straighten out Joey Wells, a teacher and the Board member's other son. Joey Wells was a middle school history teacher in the district who spent more time burnishing his reputation as a faculty room lawyer than he did working on his development as a teacher.

Joey Wells would arrive just ahead of the students in the morning, therefore taking instructional time to prepare the classroom for his lessons. He remained seated in his classroom when students passed to their specials, such as music, art, and P.E. When the student dismissal bell sounded each afternoon, Joey Wells would be out the door exactly fifteen minutes later, as per contract.

His lack of progress as a teacher and his destructive leadership among the other teachers concerned his building principal enough to call Lilly for help. Lilly helped the principal construct a professional improvement plan for Joey Wells. Failure to meet the plan's mandates would result in withholding the annual increment or dismissal. Joey Wells protested loud and long that he was being singled out.

Immediately after the improvement plan was delivered to Joey Wells, Joey's father and Board member Daniel Wells began to interrogate Lilly at public Board of Education meetings in front of the cameras. He would probe every agenda item for which she was responsible. No response from Lilly could satisfy Wells, determined as he was to embarrass her publicly. At one point he announced at a public Board meeting that "Lilly Laboy is clearly incompetent."

Lilly drove home in tears that night.

"Oh, shit," she repeated to DelVecchio on news that Daniel Wells's other son was now in trouble.

The youngest and just arrested Wells originally had joined the local fire department, but his inability to maintain the physical requirements and his constant absence from fire training, proved him unable to make it through his first year.

The president of the firefighters' union had met with DelVecchio when he was still the H.R. director, and he secured a spot for young Wells on the school district's building and grounds crew. In return, the fire union chief would agree to throw his members' support behind those Board members intent on overthrowing the new superintendent, who had gotten the job instead of DelVecchio. Her dismissal would open the door for DelVecchio's ascension.

"Have you talked to the lawyers?" Lilly asked.

"Yes," DelVecchio answered. "And I've already talked to Kaifes about the union ramifications, and to Tony about the investigation."

Deputy Police Chief Tony Martino also served as a member of the Menlo Grove Board of Education.

"Oh, and I've just gotten off the phone with Daniel Wells," DelVecchio concluded.

"What do you want me to do?" Lilly asked.

"You meet with Kaifes to determine a solution we can both live with. I'll meet with the lawyers and Bill, of course," DelVecchio said, referring to Board president Bill Burton.

"Oh, great, I've got to meet with that sleaze?"

"Would you rather meet with Poppa Wells?" DelVecchio asked.

"You know the answer to that," she said as she left his office.

No sooner had Lilly returned to her office, that her cell phone began vibrating vigorously. The phone identified the caller as her husband.

"Hi," she said.

"You won't believe this," her husband began excitedly, "I just heard from the realtor. We got an offer on the house."

"You're kidding, right? "Lilly asked. Their house in town had been on the market for nearly twelve months, and they had only gotten two low-ball offers.

"No, really, Lil. Listen, we just got an offer only ten grand below our asking price. Let's take it, Lil. Let's get out of here."

"Hold on a minute," she interrupted. "Let me think a minute."

"Think about what?" He shouted. "This is what we hoped for. Prayed for. Let's sell the place and move full time to the Shore. There is nothing to think about."

"I've got a lot going on here right now," she said calmly. "We'll talk tonight."

"Bullshit," he shouted into the phone. "We're taking this offer and moving full-time to the Shore. You want to stay here, fine. You can move in with your mom. I'm so out of here." He abruptly hung up.

Her husband's adamant tone surprised her a little and snapped Lilly back to reality. The house had been on the market for so long and her job had become so consuming for her that she had compartmentalized moving and locked it away.

One thing for sure, she knew her husband would move to the Shore house without her. He was spending more and more time down there anyway. His past infidelities were constant sores for her. If she did move in with her mom after the house sold and left him to live at the Shore without her, she felt certain her marriage would dissolve.

"Shit, shit, shit," she said aloud as she closed the cell phone.

Her secretary entered the office with a stack of paper.

"Mrs. Laboy, you need to look at this," she said. "Just arrived from the Child Study Team at South Menlo Grove High.

Lilly began sifting through the papers. Her worst fears were about to be realized.

The secretary couldn't wait to announce the news. "None of the meetings, interactions, or supplemental instruction between this particular Child Study Team and their special ed. students for the past two years have been documented."

Lilly squinted, and then closed her eyes for a second. "That means that whatever federal or state money had been used for such services will have to be returned. This is even worse than I thought."

"I know it," the secretary announced triumphantly as she left Lilly's office.

The auditors would soon be arriving to review the non-existent documentation. Beyond that, the district would be fined for failing to keep proper documentation. This could cost in the millions. The public relations nightmare made Lilly physically shudder.

"Oh, no," thought Lilly. "I don't need this right now."

The Division of Student Services had been left in even worse shape than Lilly feared when her predecessor decided to retire over the summer, and when Lilly had decided to move from Curriculum and Instruction to Student Services.

DelVecchio, at first unnerved by her suggestion to move to Student Services, was easily convinced by Lilly that she could clean up the mess in Student Services while keeping a close watch on the new guy and Curriculum and Instruction as well.

Lilly knew how much DelVecchio needed her to survive, and essentially with her in charge of both areas of the school district, he could be better protected by her. She could then have virtually total control of both general and special education.

She did not realize until now just what an insurmountable mess the department of Student Services was in.

"Be careful what you wish for," she whispered to herself.

The cell phone began vibrating on her desk again. It was her husband again.

"Oh, shit," she said aloud.

She was this close to a decision that would change not only her life, but the life of Michael DelVecchio as well.

TWELVE

THE NEW GUY

Lilly quickly found that having the new guy take over her former position in charge of Curriculum and Instruction while she focused on Student Services proved a mixed blessing. On the one hand his experience provided him the knowledge to handle the day-to-day issues without much supervision. With all the pupil services issues now confronting her, Lilly was happy no longer to have to worry about keeping the huge wheel of curriculum turning.

However, DelVecchio insisted that Lilly educate Ferrone on the nuances of Menlo Grove, that is, the political considerations that went into every decision. Therefore, after her own long day of dealing with the special education mess, late each afternoon she entered Ferrone's office to assist with his "schooling."

"How is it going?" she asked as she entered his office.

"Oh, hi, Lilly," he answered, looking up from one of three large stacks of paper sitting, like a miniature section of the Appalachian Mountains, on his desk.

"I'm just working on these requests for daily leave time. Surprised so many teachers miss instructional time to complete so much clerical work."

Lilly shrugged her shoulders. "It's in the contract. What are you going to do?" she added rhetorically. "Remember, don't alienate the union. Any questions come up today?"

"As a matter of fact, yes," Ferrone responded. "I spent quite a bit of time today trying to collect data for the State Report Card."

"Oh, God," Lucy put her right hand up to her forehead and closed her eyes in apparent pain. "We in Curriculum and Instruction refer to it as the FSRC."

"FSRC?" Ferrone asked. He knew hundreds of educational acronyms, but FSRC had somehow escaped him.

"Yes," Lilly responded. "The Fucking State Report Card."

"Oh, right," Ferrone smiled. "My secretary and I have sent emails and called all of the people responsible for the different numbers we need to complete the report before submitting it to the state, but a number of people don't know what we're talking about."

"What do you mean?" Lilly asked. She had been responsible for and completed the Fucking State Report Card during her time in charge of Curriculum and Instruction.

"Well," Ferrone continued, "some people, for example in Technology, have told me they had never been asked for these numbers before. Sam in Technology said he has never needed to supply this office with the number of computer drops in every classroom in every building. Said he could never get those numbers in time."

"Oh, that," Lucy said, waving the comment off with a wave of her hand. "If they don't have the numbers, just fudge it."

Ferrone stared incredulously at her.

She averted her eyes and kept going. "Just get it done and have your secretary send it to State Department of Ed. If the Education Department finds something that seems wrong, they will return the report, and you can correct it then."

"How do I correct fudged numbers?" he asked naively.

"Just adjust them to make them more believable," she answered calmly.

Now she knew why DelVecchio wanted her to check on Ferrone every day.

"Why not just get the real numbers?" Ferrone asked. "They exist somewhere."

"Look," Lilly answered quietly and firmly. "The amount of work you are expected to complete each day is impossible. You could stay here all day and all night every day and every night and still not get the work all done. This is a huge school district, and the most important driver of this district is curriculum."

She continued, "And do you know who is responsible for EVERYTHING getting done in curriculum?"

She didn't pause for an answer. "You are. You and you alone."

Ferrone kept staring in disbelief. 'I'll get the numbers, Lilly."

She shrugged her shoulders and left his office. "He's in for a rude awakening," she thought to herself as she trudged down the hallway to her office. She needed to search for missing documentation for supplemental services delivered to learning disabled students. Without documentation, the money the district had received from the state to pay for these services would have to be returned. Plus, the district faced the real possibility of a fine.

Ferrone, meanwhile, was also taken by surprise by another area of his responsibility: Board of Education Policy. Ferrone's secretary entered his office with the Policy and Procedures binder.

"Bertha," Ferrone asked her, "How did policy grow as an extension of Curriculum and Instruction?"

Bertha had worked in the curriculum office for ten years and, like most secretaries, knew more than what she would admit to knowing.

"When Lilly amassed more power into the curriculum office, she wanted to keep her hands on Board policy."

Ferrone smiled knowingly, but said nothing about Lilly.

"Nearly every day a policy question comes up. I don't know how Lilly did it all."

"She spent a lot of time here," Bertha answered. "But she concentrated on some things more than others."

"Yeah, not the Fucking State Report Card," Ferrone thought.

"Thanks for bringing the Policy book in. I will start searching. I cannot believe Menlo Grove still has these large binders with hard copies of the district's policy and procedure."

Ferrone continued. "Why do you think the district never put any of this information on its computers? Doesn't seem like a big deal. Policy always has to follow the state's administrative code."

"Yes," Bertha said, "but district procedures change according to political winds."

Procedures explained how a policy was enforced.

"You are very smart," Ferrone told her.

Bertha left his office with a smile on her face.

Ferrone had been shocked to discover that most of the Board's policies had not been revised in over a decade. As state codes seemingly changed monthly, it became imperative for a school district to update its policies.

This proved another area where Menlo Grove had been shortsighted. After revising policy according to current code, Ferrone's revisions were sent to the Board's private legal firm for further review. This proved expensive. The large law firm charged over $10,000 for each review.

As he revised yet another policy on early entry into kindergarten, Ferrone thought, "Perhaps the district had fallen behind in policy revision simply as a way to save some money."

He decided to make an appointment to see DelVecchio with an idea.

Ferrone entered DelVecchio's office one day soon after to propose hiring a company to review the entire policy document, which consisted of over a thousand pages, and having the company revise according to current code. He had gotten a quote of $20,000. Many districts regularly outsourced this practice.

"No," DelVecchio had brusquely answered. "We can't afford it."

"But having each new policy reviewed individually is costing the district a whole lot more," Ferrone insisted.

"Don't fix what's not broken," DelVecchio replied sternly.

"Isn't it broken?" Ferrone asked rhetorically.

With his own well-practiced game face, DelVecchio stared silently as he looked right through Ferrone.

"Discretion is the better part of valor," Ferrone thought, recalling his days of teaching Shakespeare to skinny boys and teenaged girls who didn't understand and were busy picking at their hair anyway. He said nothing but smiled at DelVecchio.

The sun had set, at each of the district's school buildings the busses had taken the students home, and the shift into the second part of Ferrone's day was beginning.

Ferrone had decided, and had told DelVecchio, that his first goal was to visit with the principal of every one of the seventeen buildings. Since he was already in DelVecchio's office, he figured it was a chance to ask if he could get started on the school visits.

"What do you think of my idea to visit each principal in her building?" Ferrone asked.

DelVecchio smiled. "I checked with Lilly about your idea of going to each building to meet with the principals," DelVecchio surprised Ferrone with the bluntness of this admission.

"I've decided that this is a good idea, but be sure you contact each principal before you show up."

"Of course," Ferrone answered.

Ferrone had already announced his plan at the first principals' meeting he had attended, but he knew DelVecchio was a stickler for detail when it came to keeping his principals happy. Therefore, Ferrone wanted to make certain DelVecchio knew all about it.

As Ferrone drove south on the state highway which intersected the town, where five of the elementary schools, two of the middle schools, and Menlo Grove South High School were located, his journey took him past the empty factories and deserted industrial parks which at one time had made Menlo Grove such a vibrant municipality.

Some of the southern part of town now served as a large, low-cost housing opportunity for the struggling, working poor. The large, barren empty parcels of land along the busy highway resembled the top of West Virginia mountaintops, which had been cut off for strip mining and left empty and exposed when the mining companies exited.

The principals who had served in the district for a long time had experienced the changing demographics in the southern part of town and the resulting decline in test scores. Some citizens who lived in the southern part of town came to Board meetings to complain against the discrimination. The test scores in the schools at the northern end were so much better; the district must be offering those schools better programs with better teachers, or so the argument went.

Ferrone rolled his eyes and shook his head as he listened the parents and retirees who attended the monthly Board meetings to complain. "They have no idea," he thought.

DelVecchio often told his administrative team during his Tuesday morning cabinet meetings, "I could switch all the teachers in the northern schools to the south, and move the teachers in the southern schools to the north, and the test scores would be exactly the same."

All sitting around the long, rectangular table would nod their heads in agreement. That is, everyone except for testing coordinator, Brenda Dredahl. She would sit silently and look down as she scribbled notes.

As he drove around the heavily congested town, Ferrone reflected on his recent experience facilitating a workshop on Professional Learning Communities in October at the state's School Board Association annual convention in Atlantic City.

At the same convention, Lilly had given a presentation on the exorbitant cost of special education to local school districts. While some general education parents yammered for charter schools, vouchers, and school choice, parents with special needs children knew that the public school system was the ONLY choice when it came to educating their children.

No politician wanted to discuss how the cost of special education was bankrupting local districts. Special education was not only the 800-pound gorilla in the room; it was the third rail of public education. Try to cut special education money and an administrator would soon be considered cold, uncaring, and targeted at public meetings.

What surprised Ferrone the most about the School Boards convention, however, was the free flow of food and alcohol during the three days. He had attended four different receptions his first day there, open to all, and sponsored by different law firms, publishing companies, and technology outfits eager to sell their wares to the schools.

"Seems a bit like bribing, don't you think?" Ferrone naively had asked Lilly during bites of shrimp and sips of gin and tonic at one of the lavish receptions.

"Don't be silly," Lilly replied. "This is a treat for Board members, who are volunteers, remember. They can be a royal pain in the ass, but for the time they put in, a few days of free food seems a fair exchange. You think private industry doesn't do this every day?"

Both Ferrone's workshop and Lilly's presentation had gone extremely well, and the Menlo Grove Board members who had attended spoke enthusiastically upon their return north on how great the two assistant superintendents had made the school district look.

The individual meetings with the principals took Ferrone a full month. The volume of paper work, as Lilly had warned, arrived non-stop from every department in every building in the school district. However, Ferrone found the principals gracious with their time as they took him on a tour of their buildings, and open in their responses to his questions.

Without fail, all the elementary principals complained that every other elementary principal had used Lilly's lack of attention and condescending attitude to the elementary schools as an excuse to move curriculum in whatever direction each individual principal saw fit.

His conversation with Cyndi Zubricki, one of the three she-wolves always trying to undermine Lucy the supervisor's attempts to unify the district's elementary curriculum, typified most of Ferrone's conversations with the elementary principals. Cyndi met Ferrone at the front door of her building.

"So good to finally see you in my building. Welcome," Zubricki said in greeting the new Assistant Superintendent.

"Cyndi, thanks for letting me visit your school. Wow, this really looks great. Very welcoming lobby."

"We do our best," Cyndi replied. "It gets more and more difficult."

"You have done wonderful work in the district, Cyndi. Can we meet somewhere to talk?"

"Sure, let me give you a short tour and then we will go to my office."

Cyndi served as principal of the smallest elementary building in the district, but her complaints more than made up for those who seldom complained though they managed much larger buildings.

Fifteen minutes later, the two long-time public school administrators sat in Zubricki's office. Her desk sat in one corner. Piles of paper sat atop the desk. She and Ferrone sat at a rectangular table in the center of the room. More piles framed the two, both in the business over thirty years.

"Cyndi, let's cut to the chase. What do you think is the biggest curriculum issue the district faces?"

"That's easy," Cyndi replied. "Every building is in a different place regarding the elementary curriculum. Some buildings follow the curriculum. Some do their own thing."

"What do you think needs to be done?"

"We need to train all the principals on the curriculum, so every building is on the same page."

Virtually every elementary principal said the same thing to Ferrone. Every principal believed that every other principal was not holding his or her teachers to the district curriculum.

"Okay, thanks, Cyndi. It sounds like I will put together some training for the principals. I will work with Lucy on this," Ferrone smiled at Zubricki.

Cyndi did not return the smile.

The principals knew how overwhelmed Lilly was with all her work at central office, so they knew if Lucy complained about the principals not following the district curriculum with Lilly, she would have no time to do anything about it. No one would ever excuse Lilly Laboy of not having a work ethic, but as she had told Ferrone, the mountains of paper arriving in the Curriculum and Instruction office every day proved impossible to complete.

Ferrone discovered that the principals also felt elementary supervisor Lucy Williams had tried to move all the elementary principals in one direction, but she lacked the authority. Lilly ran the show; everyone acknowledged that. And Lilly did not share authority with anyone.

Lilly would listen to Lucy, nod, and apparently agree. However, Lucy knew that keeping peace with the principals was more important to DelVecchio than forcing them to have a consistent district-wide curriculum. The decision was easy.

After each meeting with a principal, Ferrone became more determined that supervisor Lucy Williams served as the key to develop training for the principals so those principals not well versed in elementary instruction would all have the same template for evaluating its delivery. Certainly, some of the high school people who had been assigned to the elementary schools were not well versed at all.

There were a few of the elementary principals, including the three she-wolves, who did possess expertise, and Ferrone decided he would use them as well to facilitate the training. "Keep your friends close, and your enemies closer," he thought.

"Seems like a win-win," he thought as he drove north on the state highway, past the central office to the left and into the more affluent section of town, with its sparkling and expansive Ford City Mall on one side of the highway, and the upscale Woodrow Wilson Park Mall on the other.

When he returned to his office late in the afternoon, there was a message on his machine from Lilly Laboy and one from testing coordinator Brenda Dredahl. He decided to call Dredahl first.

"What's up?"

"The state scores just arrived," she began, obviously upset. "This is not good," she continued.

"Okay, give it to me straight," Ferrone said calmly. He had been through the test score war many times before.

Under No Child Left Behind, every group of children, regardless of learning disability, minority status, or economic disadvantage, had to achieve a certain benchmark.

There were two problems with this. First, a child was not measured against how he or she had scored previously, but how a group of different children had scored the previous year. Second, the benchmark score was raised every other year. In other words, even if a larger percentage of children achieved a passing score one year, the percentage of children passing was continually raised until eventually, in the very near future, 100% of the children in every group would be expected to attain a passing score. The system was set up for failure, as if someone wanted to prove that public schools did not work.

"Menlo Grove South High did not achieve the benchmark. Again," Dredahl's voice now quivered in anger. "Again," she repeated. "After all the money we spent on the supplemental instruction, after all the additional training for the teachers, after all those expensive programs we bought with the federal money."

"Oh, boy," Ferrone exhaled. "Does that mean what I think it does?" he asked

Dredahl.

Since he was new to the district, he wanted to be certain.

"Yes, it does," she said.

"School choice," he muttered sotto voce, almost afraid someone might hear.

"Absolutely," she said. "Do you know how many parents are going to want to transfer their little angels to Henry Ford High?" she asked rhetorically.

"What a nightmare," Ferrone said. "Does DelVecchio know?"

"Yes, I already talked to him," she replied. "He is upset," she understated the obvious. "He had Principal Applegate on the phone immediately."

Sam Applegate had returned to his alma mater as principal of the troubled high school in the southern part of town. After the Acting Superintendent, the principal would be the next target of the irate parents, who were sending their children to a school on the dreaded "failing school list."

Under the law, if a school failed to achieve the ever-raised bar for a certain number of years consecutively, even if those who failed to achieve were just a small number of learning disabled children, the entire school was placed in the category "Failing School" and students in that school had the option of transferring to another school within that district.

Because the demographic of Henry Ford High School was so much different, so much more affluent, than Menlo Grove South High School, Henry Ford High School's scores were much better. The parents might very well flee from Menlo Grove South High, and flock to Henry Ford, which was already bursting at the seams.

"Okay, I'll get back to you," Ferrone hung up the phone, leaned back in his chair, and whistled under his breath.

He then checked a voicemail left by Lilly.

"Please come to my office as soon as you arrive," the messages said in Lilly's trembling voice. "I want to tell you something."

Ferrone immediately rose from his chair to walk to Lilly's office down the hall.

"Things seem to be going well until a minute ago. I wonder what she wants?" he thought.

Michael Ferrone had no idea at that moment what Lilly was about to tell him, and that everything in the Menlo

Grove school district was about to undergo a dramatic change. When Lilly told Ferrone she made the decision to retire, he would be faced with a situation that caused him to question the very role of public education in American society.

THIRTEEN

THE INTERVIEW COMMITTEE

Lilly greeted the members of the interview committee as they entered the small windowless room with the large table. The setting was the same as when Michael Ferrone had been interviewed just a few months earlier.

The news of Lilly's sudden decision to retire from public education and join her husband at their home at the Shore spread rapidly through the large district. The old timers were not entirely shocked, especially with the news regarding the sale of her home in town.

"Thank you for agreeing to serve on this committee. We will be interviewing six candidates for the position of Assistant Superintendent of Student Services," Lilly began.

Ferrone glanced at each of the faces sitting around the table. At first he thought it unusual that the person being replaced would chair the committee choosing the replacement. However, even after just a few months in Menlo Grove, he understood that DelVecchio, shaken as he was by Lilly's decision to retire, needed to keep a firm grip on the process. Ferrone also recalled that Lilly had, of course, chaired the committee that had chosen him to replace her in C & I.

"The prospective candidates have been chosen through the personnel department's screening process," Lilly continued without a trace of irony in her voice.

Everyone at the table knew that DelVecchio had agreed to continue as Director of Personnel upon his sudden ascension as Acting Superintendent. What most at the table did not realize, however, was that the screening process was not completed by DelVecchio, but by Lilly herself.

After the personnel secretary had eliminated those candidates without proper certification, the most promising remaining candidates had been selected by Lilly. She cleared each of the six to be interviewed with DelVecchio. He wrote a short note to himself about each of the selections, indicating the political ramifications for each if chosen.

The people chosen to serve on the committee sat around the table. Lilly and DelVecchio had decided those who would sit on the committee. They included Grace Romanczak, principal of Henry Ford High School; Brenda Dredahl, testing coordinator, whose presence on these committees illustrated the importance standardized testing had gained; the Union Boss's first assistant, who taught middle school social studies; the ubiquitous elementary principal Rosemary Grogan-Unangst, who seemed to serve on every interview committee; and Ferrone. Lilly would be the sixth member.

Like a test proctor reading directions to a state test at students in a room, Lilly presented directions to the committee members. "A list of questions has been distributed to each of you. Look over the questions and choose one to ask. Score the response for each question asked from 1 to 5."

"Do we use the pencil in front of us?" the union guy asked. This was his first experience on an interview committee.

"Yes, please," Lilly responded. "Mark your scores in pencil. I will collect the score sheets at the conclusion of each interview."

"Acting Superintendent DelVecchio has decided to forego the several rounds of interviews," she continued. "This committee's recommendation will be brought directly to Mr. DelVecchio."

Ferrone thought about the several rounds of interviews he had experienced. He wondered why the change in process.

Lilly continued as if she read Ferrone's mind. "The position of Assistant Superintendent for Student Services needs to be replaced as quickly as possible. The division cannot possibly be without leadership because of all the impending litigation."

The special education mess that Lilly had uncovered and was leaving behind for her replacement made DelVecchio nervous enough. His cigarette consumption had nearly doubled with Lilly's retirement announcement.

Ferrone found DelVecchio's decision to forego the second round interesting, however. A position as important as Assistant Superintendent for Student Services dealt with the dangers inclusive of special education. For example, with the exorbitant costs and the potential for lawsuits, the idea of bringing in a wide range of stakeholders, such as someone to represent the parents, someone with solid experience in special education, and someone with legal expertise, seemed common sense to Ferrone.

None of those descriptions fit the people sitting around the table.

DelVecchio's need to control the process seemed like an obvious act of desperation and failure to trust the judgment of those stakeholders. Top-down decision-making contained short term haste and long term regret.

Lilly continued, "Three of the candidates for the position are from inside the district and three come from school districts in the north and central parts of the state." Each interview will take forty-five minutes for our questioning, and I will escort the candidate out after the interview concludes. We will then discuss the candidate for ten minutes. After that, I bring in the next candidate, and we will repeat the process. Are there any questions before we begin?"

When no one responded to her inquiry, Lilly continued, "We'll break for lunch after the third candidate, and then do the last three interviews after lunch. I will identify our top candidate to Mr. DelVecchio and then contact the candidate. That person will meet with Mr. DelVecchio soon after."

"What if he doesn't like our first choice?" Ferrone asked, curious if he had been the committee's first choice and the only one to meet with DelVecchio.

"The Acting Superintendent will have the final decision, but in the past he has followed the committee's recommendations," Lilly answered.

"But this time there is only one round," thought Ferrone, "and no one here is an expert on special education." He kept this thought to himself.

As the day progressed, each candidate entered the room wide-eyed and totally alone, dressed in a dark suit, nervous but savvy enough to get through the round of questioning. The process moved forward just as Lilly had described. At the end of the long day, Lilly began by reading each candidate's score aloud.

The three in-house candidates finished with the highest scores. The top two were both grizzled veterans of the district, each with over twenty years of experience. One was a current middle school principal and one a supervisor.

The top two candidates were both typical of the veteran Menlo Grove staff: graduates of the school district, each with a relative who either had or was still employed by the district, with ancestry traced to Western Europe. That is, white. They did not reflect the current make up of the student population, 60% of which was non-white and of Asian or Hispanic descent. The third candidate was a young woman of Asian descent who grew up in a nearby district.

A short discussion followed Lilly's reading of the names and scores.

"I think our top candidate has enough experience to do the job," said the principal of Henry Ford High, Grace Romanczak.

"Well, I agree to a point," added testing coordinator Dredahl. "But we have no hard evidence that he will be able to raise the test scores of the average special ed student in the district."

"Average special ed student? What the hell does that mean?" asked Ferrone.

"All the candidates did very well. Lilly did a great job of screening," noted elementary principal and ever charming she-wolf representative Grogan-Unangst.

The union guy was on his phone, texting the Union Boss the results of the scoring.

"Okay, then," Lilly announced. "I will bring Mr. DelVecchio the name of our top candidate. Thank you for investing the day to help in securing the best candidate for the district. I have enjoyed working with all of you during my long tenure here in Menlo Grove, which is one of the finest districts in the state."

Before the room emptied, each committee member moved toward Lilly and offered kind words of gratitude for her work and shared their envy for her decision to walk away from the craziness.

When everyone had left, Lilly gathered all the papers strewn atop the table.

When she entered the Acting Superintendent's office, union boss Kristoff Kaifes was already sitting at the round table next to DelVecchio. DelVecchio was just hanging up the phone.

"The committee has chosen Dan O'Dowd, principal at JFK Middle School," she stated.

"I know that," DelVecchio said.

Kaifes smiled wanly at Lilly.

"So what do you think?" Lilly asked.

'Who came in second?" DelVecchio asked.

"Uh," Lilly hesitated. She was not expecting that question. "Um, Shirley Eckhardt, Social Studies supervisor."

"And how about third?" DelVecchio stated as if reading from a script.

"My God," Lilly wondered. "Is he going to ask for all six scores?" She looked at her list. "A young woman named Abha Patel. She is a special education teacher with ten years of experience. She belongs to a number of county committees on special education issues. She grew up in Bridgetown, the next district to our north."

"I know where Bridgetown is," DelVecchio answered calmly.

"Of course he does," thought Lilly, embarrassed. She knew DelVecchio had lived his entire life in Menlo Grove and knew the entire county intimately.

"Okay, I want to see the top three candidates," DelVecchio said. "Set up fifteen -minute meetings for each of them. Get them in here tomorrow. I am busy and don't have much time for all this."

"Okay, no problem," Lilly said. "Why do you want to see the top three?"

Union boss Kaifes shifted in his seat. Lilly realized he already knew the answer.

"Menlo Grove needs to better reflect our constituency, I mean, our population. I want to talk to all three candidates to see who might be the best fit," DelVecchio responded calmly. "Are they all qualified to be Assistant Superintendent?"

"Of course they're all qualified," Lilly replied. "I did the screening myself. Everyone we interviewed holds all the proper certifications and is totally able to do the job. And it is a big, big job awaiting this next person. Patel, however, is still just a teacher."

"You just said they could all do the job. Can she?" DelVecchio asked impatiently.

Lilly responded instantly, "She does have experience with the major issues."

Her raised voice belied her resentment. She felt happy she would soon be leaving all this. Kaifes sat quietly. Lilly wondered what he was thinking. She wondered why he was even in the room. "Never alienate the union," she thought to herself.

"I want you to work with whomever I choose as your replacement. Will you be able to stay on for an extra month to break in the new person?" DelVecchio asked.

"Yes, sure. Of course," she responded. "The house closing will take quite awhile to happen. We have to get everything in the house packed and either moved, stored, or thrown away. I have some time."

"Okay, then," DelVecchio concluded. "Call the three finalists and have my secretary set up appointments for tomorrow. Thank you."

Lilly remained a bit perplexed as she exited DelVecchio's office. Suddenly she felt like she couldn't wait for the day when she would drive south on the freeway across the bridge leading to the Shore and never look back at Menlo Grove.

As she turned the corner of the hallway and walked away, Board president Bill Burton entered the building via the side door, which was supposed to be a fire exit only. He walked straight into the office of the Acting Superintendent, which Lilly had just left.

Lilly may have decided to leave Menlo Grove behind for the warmth of the Shore, but the wheels of the machine would continue to turn. The ending of tenure for superintendents was meant to keep the decision-making process more focused on what was best for the district. Without tenure, a superintendent could be replaced after the contract ended. Or, in the case of Menlo Grove, bought out in the middle of a contract.

However, even the purest of intentions at some point must collide with the reality of human nature. The Acting Superintendent, the Union Boss, and the Board president were about meet and to make a decision based not on what was best for the education of the district's children, but on the best political option to secure the Acting Superintendent another contract.

FOURTEEN

THE ACTING SUPERINTENDENT

Two weeks earlier, Lilly had walked into Michael DelVecchio's office at 8:02 A.M. The acting superintendent, surprised to see her at such an early hour, offered his usual gruff nicotine enhanced greeting, "Good Morning."

"I have decided to retire," Lilly abruptly announced.

"But you just months ago took over the division of student services," DelVecchio really thought she was kidding.

Lilly immediately began sobbing. He knew at that moment she was serious.

"Lilly, what are you doing?" DelVecchio, who had never seen her even mist up before, asked with desperation in his voice.

"You and I are a team. We take no prisoners."

She began tearfully gulping out the reasons for her sudden decision to retire.

DelVecchio's eyes grew large, but he sat in silence.

His mind raced, however. "What would Lilly's leaving would mean to my chances at a new contract," he thought to himself.

That was two weeks ago.

Today Lilly arrived in DelVecchio's office at 10:20 A.M., a few days after she, DelVecchio, and Union Boss Kaifes discussed the interviews for Lilly's replacement.

DelVecchio's head was resting on his hand as he read the morning newspaper lying flat on his desk.

"Have you talked to the top candidates to replace me," she asked.

DelVecchio looked up from the newspaper.

"I have," DelVecchio replied without looking up. I plan to call Bill this morning," he replied quietly. This had left DelVecchio with another quandary he had not anticipated.

Bill Burton, the Board of Education president, needed to be chosen as president in the spring following every Board election and public vote on the budget.

DelVecchio's cell phone call had Burton on speed dial.

After Lilly had told DelVecchio she had decided she had had enough of Menlo Grove, he called Burton as soon as Lilly had left his office.

"Lilly has decided to retire. What am I going to do?" DelVecchio growled into the phone.

Board president Bill Burton seemed unperturbed. "I'll be right over," he said.

Ten minutes later the Board president was sitting at the round table in DelVecchio's office. "Who do you have in mind for Lilly's replacement?"

"I have no idea," DelVecchio muttered. "This really fucks things up."

Burton continued, "For the next Board election, we need to broaden our voting constituency. The opposition on the blogs looks like they are organizing to run a block of candidates opposing the three incumbents running for reelection. All three incumbents support giving you a new contract. Last year there were so many opposition candidates they splintered all the votes, and we were able to keep your majority intact for the most part."

"Yeah, for the most part," DelVecchio repeated sarcastically. "How about Larry and Suzee?" DelVecchio reminded Burton of the two Board members who consistently spoke out against the current administration.

"Those two actually help, in a way," Burton explained analytically. "Having a couple of dissenting voices on the Board makes the process seem more democratic."

"If all three of the incumbents get defeated this time, however," DelVecchio broke in, "then there will be five dissenting voices, and you know what that means."

"It means we're fucked. That's why we need to get some new voters out to the polls who like what the school district is doing."

"How do you propose to do that? You know the newer immigrants in town don't vote in great numbers," DelVecchio said.

They had studied the voting demographics within the town's precincts and the registration rolls. Some neighborhoods participated in the voting process in unbelievably small numbers, even during general elections. During the April Board of Education elections for school budgets and Board members, the numbers were miniscule.

"We need to get a high-profile Asian face representing the district," Burton declared. "That could counteract all the negativity boiling up on the blogs. Plus, it would make us seem less like we were out to get the mayor. We cannot have the Asian voters think we are against our Korean-American mayor."

"I'll have Lilly put an interview committee together for her replacement. But I cannot guarantee who will apply for that job," DelVecchio said.

"What about Patel, the teacher? I heard good things about her," Burton stated.

"She's only been a teacher here for ten years, Bill. She needs more time."

"We don't have more time, Mike. You want a new contract, don't you?"

DelVecchio put on his game face. "You know I do. No one can run this district like I can."

"Then you need to get your three incumbents reelected. And we need more Asian votes," Burton made it all so simple.

"Okay," DelVecchio said. "I'll take care of it."

Now Lilly and the committee had completed the interviews and had decided on a top candidate. The phone rang in DelVecchio's office. It was testing coordinator Brenda Dredahl.

"Mr. DelVecchio," she began, in her measured military tone. "I just received the state test results, and there is bad news."

"Have you spoken to the new guy yet?" DelVecchio asked. Test results belonged in the domain of Curriculum and Instruction.

"No. You told me you wanted to see test results as soon as they arrived. I did leave his secretary a message. He is out flitting around, visiting with building principals, still on his "listening tour" of the district.

"Okay," DelVecchio said, "what's the bottom line?"

"Menlo Grove South High has failed to meet the benchmarks for special education. Again," she practically shouted into the phone. "No AYP!"

"Meaning?" DelVecchio had trouble connecting the dots.

"Meaning they did not make their AYP – Annual Yearly Progress. That means school choice. The students at Menlo South High School can choose to transfer to Henry Ford High School," she stated emphatically.

"How can the state expect us to fit all those students whose parents want them to transfer? We have more than 2,000 students crowding into each high school. What if 1,000 students from Menlo Grove South decide to transfer to Henry Ford?"

"The state doesn't care," Dredahl said. DelVecchio could clearly visualize her chin and nose rise in the air as she sniffed out her response.

"All because a few special ed students did not pass the state test, we could have to suddenly transfer a thousand kids all the way uptown? Make new schedules? Arrange new bus routes? How do we schedule classes for students without enough rooms? Does the state expect us to transfer teachers, too?"

"The state doesn't care," she repeated.

DelVecchio's next call was to the principal of Menlo Grove South High School.

Sam Applegate, the current principal at Menlo Grove South High School, had been a high school hero in his own right when he was a student at Menlo Grove South. The Applegate family had a long history in Menlo Grove. Sam's father had been mayor of the town in the early 1960s, long before the demographics had changed, and Sam's mother had been a home economics teacher at the high school.

"What the fuck is going on down there?" DelVecchio screamed into the phone when Applegate picked up.

'What? What is it, Mr. DelVecchio?" Applegate still called his former phys. ed. teacher and football coach Mr. DelVecchio, despite being only ten years apart in age. Sam Applegate was in his mid-50s, but still acted like a frightened 15-year old in DelVecchio's presence.

DelVecchio knew this and used it.

"Your goddamn special ed scores did not meet the benchmark again," DelVecchio growled.

"Mr. D., we gave those kids extra classes, after school help, summer extended school year. They have cost the district so much extra money it makes my head spin. We can't do more than we're doing. They're learning disabled, for God's sake. Some of them simply aren't going to pass an eleventh grade test."

"They've got to pass the test," DelVecchio responded.

Applegate was pleading now. "Have you ever seen that test? Some of our Board members couldn't pass it."

"Doesn't matter," DelVecchio answered. "Our Board members don't have to pass it. Our special ed students do. Your job is to get them to pass it."

"Come on, be realistic. You know I'm your favorite principal," Applegate teased. Come on, Coach."

"Listen to me, Sam. Listen good." DelVecchio was about to go on a roll. "You got this job because of your name and your old man. If we had the nepotism law the state wants us to pass, you would still be teaching history to eighth grade girls in that little district at half the salary to what we're paying you we when we brought you back here."

DelVecchio continued, "Every one of my principals wants to be my favorite. I got three middle aged hags at the elementary schools calling me every morning and then again every afternoon to tell me how many second graders got dropped off late for school, that the tater tots being served for lunch are soggy, and that the elementary supervisor is being too demanding."

"Well, I don't know what else I can do," Applegate answered truthfully.

"Some Board members are going to have an idea of what to do with you," DelVecchio's voice sounded threatening. "If you can't get them to pass, I will find a principal who will."

"Good, you do that," Applegate did not appreciate getting backed into a corner. "You find a fucking principal who can get learning disabled kids to pass the test in the numbers the state is expecting. Fine, I'll retire. I don't give a fuck."

Applegate, like everyone else in the district, had heard of Lilly's announcement to retire, and knew his remark would hit DelVecchio hard with the idea that his self-selected "championship" team was abandoning ship. Applegate could afford to retire. He possessed his own version of AYP. Not Annual Yearly Progress, like the state tests. Applegate's version of AYP meant he had accumulated Age, Years, and a Passport.

Any public educator over 55 years of age had the age; if that person had been in the business for twenty-five years, they had the years; and if they liked to travel, they had a passport. AYP to many public educators in the state had nothing to do with Annual Yearly Progress on state testing. It simply meant Age, Years, and a Passport. See you later. I'm taking my pension and running.

Having age and years meant being fully vested in the pension fund. A nice check in the mail the first of the month for the rest of their lives. Applegate had the age, he had the years, and he did, in fact, have a passport. The passport was an inside joke to the educators. Still young enough and with the money and time to travel.

DelVecchio considered offering Applegate to the Board as a viable scapegoat for the problems at Menlo Grove South High School and force his retirement. The voting public could see the DelVecchio was fixing the problem by firing the principal. The Board would respond to the public's approval of a change in principal at the troubled high school. This would make DelVecchio look like a strong leader who would fire one of his own former players for the good of the district. Maybe this could work for DelVecchio after all.

"Listen, Sam," DelVecchio said calmly. "These test scores are going to hit the newspapers in a day or two. If a reporter calls you, say nothing. Direct the call to my office. You are to make no comments."

"Okay," Applegate replied. "What else do you need me to do?"

"Set up a parents' meeting. This failure to meet the benchmarks means we have to offer school choice," DelVecchio explained.

"Good," Applegate answered sarcastically. "Can I choose the students to transfer to that country club high school on the north side of town?"

DelVecchio ignored him. "Set up a meeting. Have your head of guidance there. I will send Dredahl down to explain the logistics and the law.

"Are you going to be there?" Applegate asked.

DelVecchio did not hesitate in his answer, "No fucking way. I'll send the new guy."

He hung up the phone.

DelVecchio rubbed his forehead and took a deep breath. "I need a smoke," he thought to himself as he stood up and walked out of his office.

"I'll be right back," he said to his secretary as he made his way out of the emergency exit door on the side of the building and into his district-supplied SUV. He had a cigarette in his mouth and lit before he put the key into the ignition.

Twenty minutes later, DelVecchio returned to the central office with a cup of coffee in his hand, which was shaking slightly. His secretary immediately said, without looking up from her keyboard, "Dan needs to see you right away."

DelVecchio made his way through his office door and walked into Business Administrator Dan Maris's office. A door, like in adjacent hotel rooms, connected the two offices. Most of the time the door connecting the two offices stayed open.

"What's going on?" DelVecchio asked.

"We just got the numbers from the state capital," Maris said, twitching perceptibly at what he was about to say.

"And?" DelVecchio's patience was wearing thin.

"We are going to get ten million less in state aid next year."

What little color remained in DelVecchio's face disappeared. "What? That's impossible. How can the Governor give us ten million dollars less? We're underfunded already. That prick. He's killing the suburban school districts. Those are the voters who got him elected. The urban schools are getting all the money."

Maris had heard DelVecchio rant and rave about being underfunded before. The district never got the money it should have from the state. The urban districts were getting most of the money. But those facts had nothing to do with reality. More had to be done with less.

DelVecchio wasn't done. "We're expected to get all these special ed students to pass these state tests, and the state keeps giving us less and less money."

"That's right," Maris always agreed with DelVecchio. It was easier that way.

"Let me get our state senator on the phone. Someone has got to talk sense to the Governor."

"I agree," Maris nodded again.

The phone call to the state senator proved unproductive. Politics was politics, she explained, and the Governor was getting major political mileage out of attacking the ineffective public school system.

The teachers' union was a favorite target for the governor. If he had decided to go after the police or the firefighters' unions, that would have shown bravery. But the governor was too smart for that. The teachers were mostly women. They were an easy target. No one had courage to confront the Governor, who was now getting speaking engagements in distant, much more conservative states, for standing up to the teachers' unions.

"The unions made this town," DelVecchio reminded the Senator, who represented Menlo Grove's district, and whose office was located in the town.

"Whatever works politically, Michael," she said. "You're a big boy. You know that. Don't expect any additional state funding. Everyone is going to have to make it work," she said. "Nice talking to you." And she hung up.

"I need to talk to Lilly," DelVecchio decided. "She'll know what to do." He had forgotten she had taken the day off to work on getting the house packed up and a head start on her new life.

His secretary reminded him that Lilly was not at work today. "Shit," he said aloud. "Get me the new guy."

The clock read 4:52 P.M. when Michael Ferrone walked into DelVecchio's office with his ever-present pad and pen. "I heard about the test scores," Ferrone said. "Do we have a plan?"

"Yes," DelVecchio said. "Applegate is going to meet with parents about the school choice thing. I want you to represent me at the meeting. Call Applegate in the morning."

"Okay. Anything else?" Ferrone inquired.

"We've got a major budget problem for next year. The Governor is slashing our funding again. And with our additional personnel costs because of the teachers' contract, we need to find ten million dollars. What do you have in curriculum?"

"Damn, Mike," Ferrone began. "Nothing approaching that much money. Something big is going to have to be cut. Something real big. What non-mandated program does the district offer that accounts for big bucks? Has the district added some big programs in the last few years during the gravy train days?"

"Just full-day kindergarten," DelVecchio answered.

"Well, we can't get rid of that," Ferrone said.

"Tell me why not," DelVecchio responded.

"This is mostly a working class town, Mike. You know that better than anyone. Hell, you offer pre-K for the special ed and economically disadvantaged. What are you going to do, have full day pre-K and then a half-day kindergarten? Besides, we'd have to revise all the first and second grade curricula to add the stuff the kids are doing in full day kindergarten now. Lucy Williams would have a fit."

"I can't worry about Lucy Williams having a fit. She's your problem," DelVecchio said.

"Well, your elementary principals would also go through the roof if you cut full day kindergarten," Ferrone added.

"Shit, they would," DelVecchio rubbed his forehead again.

"Okay, what else could we cut?" he asked Ferrone.

"Most everything big is mandated. I mean we're not even meeting the state mandate on elementary world language now because we're not offering it until third grade. State says we must have a K-12 world language program."

"Fuck the state," DelVecchio was growling again. "They want K-12 world language, they can pay for it. We'll cut the world language until the kids get to middle school."

"That won't be even close to ten million," Ferrone said. "It's not even one million."

"We could get rid of half the elementary world language teachers. That's real money. And we could pick up quite a few classrooms if we go to half-day kindergarten. The elementary principals would love getting rid of those elementary world language teachers who couldn't make it dealing with the high school kids, and they would really love having the additional classrooms we'd get from only having kindergarten half-day."

"But some of those awful world language teachers are also elementary certified, and would bump our newer elementary classroom teachers," Ferrone reminded him. "Seniority rights. They've been in the district forever. You can get rid of the world language program, but you would have to keep some of those teachers. We'd be losing some very good young teachers because of bumping rights."

"You're supposed to be helping me here," DelVecchio said. "I need solutions from you."

Ferrone remembered what Lilly had told him on his first day. "Your primary job is to protect the Superintendent."

He winced at the thought. Education was not his top priority. Protecting the Superintendent was. How could he have forgotten?

"Let me work on some things, Mike. I'll look at the entire program and we'll talk again."

"By end of business tomorrow," DelVecchio said. "Thank you."

That meant the meeting was over.

DelVecchio sat alone in his office. The secretaries were long gone, leaving at 4:00. The night custodian could be heard vacuuming far down the long hallway. The educator with almost forty-five years of experience thought back at the events that led to his sitting in the superintendent's big office.

A few years ago, Luigi Marinelli, DelVecchio's former coaching colleague and mentor, had decided to retire as Superintendent of the Menlo Grove Public Schools, and he had announced that Claire Smith would be his recommendation to the Board as his successor. The reaction to this startling news around the district could only be described as stunned.

Everyone, including DelVecchio, expected DelVecchio to become the next Superintendent. Indeed, the conventional wisdom had been that was the primary reason DelVecchio had been moved to the central office in the first place.

The plan seemed simple enough. DelVecchio had been a teacher and coach, chairman of the P.E. department, athletic director, vice principal, then principal of one of the middle schools. The move to the central office as Director of Human Resources made sense. DelVecchio could learn the ways of the central office; he already knew the town and the district better than anyone. After a year or two, when Marinelli announced his retirement, DelVecchio could slip right into place. The long career in public education and his loyalty to the school system and the town would culminate in the ultimate reward: the superintendency.

The position of Superintendent carried many perks: a car, five weeks of vacation days, sick days, good salary, and the power to recommend to the Board of Education every potential employee. The state had eliminated tenure for Superintendents, but that had just the opposite effect of its intent: Superintendents now had no reason to stay in a district.

Instead, Superintendents would sign a contract, either a three or five-year deal, and immediately begin planning for their next contract often at another district. Districts would bid against one another for an ever-decreasing pool of qualified candidates. Unfortunately for the local Boards of Education and the local taxpayers, the free market system was working just the way it was supposed to.

The salary of a Superintendent had increased tremendously. However, the job of Superintendent had become 24-7 for twelve months a year. The juggling of the finance with the governance, and the crumbling facilities because of deferred maintenance, the transportation and special education issues, the incredibly large number of personnel, the ever-expanding legal issues with their costs, putting together a budget that could pass the public vote every spring, the union demands, and the Board of Ed members who thought themselves preening politicos had broken many former educators who thought they wanted to run a district. The issues of curriculum and instruction, the primary purpose of public education, seemed too often to be a secondary issue, at best, when it came to decision-making.

In most communities, the school district was the largest business in town - with more employees and a bigger budget than any other enterprise in a community. Add to that the fact that one dealt with citizens' most precious possessions, their children, made the job nearly impossible. The federal government and the state politicians continually added more and more accountability standards to be met. In the case of state testing, where every student, even those with learning disabilities had to pass the tests, had made the game ultimately unwinnable.

Still, DelVecchio never even considered looking to maneuver himself for a larger contract in another district. He was embedded in Menlo Grove, and Menlo Grove was intimately part of his identity. Underlings could handle what he didn't know about curriculum or instruction. He knew the politics of the place. He was the natural next choice as Superintendent of Schools.

But another unforeseen problem of eliminating tenure, and one that did affect DelVecchio, was every Superintendent would listen to every suggestion, however uninformed, from Board members during that Superintendent's final year of a contract. This change often paralyzed progress in the school district or made for some head-scratching decision-making.

DelVecchio was irked and impatient at his predecessor's reluctance to retire, and he began wandering the central office looking for allies. He would stop by anyone's office for someone who would listen to him whine. Superintendent Marinelli, of course, heard about all this, office politics being what it is, and told DelVecchio to knock it off. His time would come.

However, what concerned Superintendent Marinelli just as much as what the gossiping DelVecchio was doing was how little DelVecchio cared to learn about running a school district except for the politics. He would miss meetings on instructional issues, have his human resources secretarial staff do all the resume screening, certification checking, interview notifying, even the putting together of committees. Some saw DelVecchio's decision to have committees choose the candidates as a brilliant idea of getting stakeholders involved. Marinelli saw the truth.

DelVecchio began the process of having committees choose recommended candidates because he soon realized just how little he did know about either curriculum or instruction. If there were a relative, friend, or someone the Board wanted hired, he could handle that. However, the years as a P.E. teacher, athletic director, and chair of the P.E. department did not exactly make him an expert in much more than multiple strategies on keeping 30-40 students busy for twenty-minutes of dodge ball, plus five minutes for students to get ready for class, five minutes for lining up and attendance, and ten minutes for students to clean up for their next class.

Even when Marinelli urged DelVecchio to learn more about the processes needed to run a large district, DelVecchio would assure him that as a lifelong resident of the town and a veteran of the district, he knew enough. If the sun was shining, or sometimes even if the sun was not, DelVecchio sometimes wouldn't return after a long lunch at the local diner. Instead, he would enjoy a round of afternoon golf with a couple of Board members, maybe the Director of Building and Business Administrator.

One spring morning, Marinelli called DelVecchio to his office, and he informed his protégé that the recommendation for the next superintendent would be going to Claire Smith, current elementary school principal. DelVecchio sat in the Superintendent's office dumbfounded. Stunned, he instantly began to plot his next move to get what was properly his to get. A coach always needs a backup plan, and DelVecchio knew the political maneuverings necessary. Claire Smith was given a three-year contract. DelVecchio became determined that she would not even survive two.

His public demeanor could not have been more professional after the decision to appoint Claire Smith superintendent was approved 5-4 by a cantankerous and split Board of Education. But behind the scenes DelVecchio plotted with the four dissenting voters to get one of the five approving members voted out of office in the following spring's Board election.

With the help of the teachers', police, and fire unions in town, enough votes could be gathered to defeat one Board member and have new Superintendent Smith put on leave for the remainder of her contract. The Board would still have to pay her, but money could always be found somewhere.

In fact, that is exactly what occurred in Menlo Grove. The first spring of Smith's short tenure as Superintendent would end as two Board members who approved her as Superintendent were voted out of office and replaced by two DelVecchio supporters. The three unions had delivered the necessary votes.

Three months later, during a July Board meeting with only one custodian, two union reps, a couple of retired guys from town, and two security guards in attendance, Claire Smith was told she was being put on leave and should no longer report to work. Michael DelVecchio, currently Director of Human Resources, would immediately replace Smith with the title of Acting Superintendent. That title would continue until Smith's contract expired in about two years. The cost to the taxpayers to keep Smith at home for the next twenty months: about half a million dollars including benefits.

The vote to put Smith on leave was approved 6-3. The vote to name DelVecchio as her replacement: 6-3.

Now, as these reflections ran through his head, DelVecchio wondered if it had been worth all the trouble if he couldn't get himself a new contract. He possessed an inexplicable need before his career concluded to be called Superintendent rather than Acting Superintendent. He wasn't sure how it would all play out. But he was sure of one thing. Michael DelVecchio had achieved his goal of running the district.

No, how it happened wasn't pretty, but even an ugly win was still a win.

Any coach could tell you that.

FIFTEEN

THE MAYOR'S OFFICE

Four town council members stood in front of the mayor. They represented a minority of the entire council, but each member present had strong support from the unions in the last election cycle.

Council member Rosie Ravioli spoke for the group. "Mr. Mayor, we are here to tell you that the party will offer a primary challenger."

She spoke solemnly, though her nervousness appeared evident. "We think you should announce that you are not running for re-election and save the town the bitterness and the cost of a primary."

"This is about the police, isn't it?" Mayor Kim asked rhetorically. "Just because I have chosen not to replace six policemen by attrition, you come to me with this bogus idea about a primary challenge?"

"This is not just about the police. A number of people believe you put together whatever constituency you have left to defeat the school referendum just to make Michael DelVecchio look bad. And a primary challenge is not a bogus idea," Ravioli responded.

"These are not layoffs. This is subtraction by attrition," the mayor raised his voice. "We have no money. And the people in town know that. And Rosie, I could not put together a constituency to defeat the school referendum. The referendum was defeated by 2-1."

"The people who think you need a primary challenger don't see it that way," she continued. "We think you should announce you're not running."

"I am running and will win re-election."

"Suit yourself, but remember, we belong to the same party as you do. You have lost our support. You have lost the support of the unions. You cannot win."

"And who will run against me in this primary?" The mayor asked.

"I will," answered Rosie Ravioli.

Ravioli, another lifelong resident of Menlo Grove, had spent most of her adult life as a homemaker who raised four children. She got involved in local politics only after her youngest child left for college. Her husband, now retired, served as a plant manager for a now closed manufacturing firm in town. The company had moved all its manufacturing overseas.

Mayor Kim knew Ravioli was right about his loss of support from the unions, but he made his case to the group standing in front of him. "I won election as mayor with a message of change for Menlo Grove. You all know that the closing of the manufacturing plants in town and influx of the newly arrived immigrants gave credence to my message of transition. You were to be my partners in that transition."

"Mister Mayor," Ravioli countered, "Once in office, many of those who voted for you suddenly realized the loss of the corporate tax base meant less revenue for the town."

"They didn't realize that before they voted for me?" he asked.

"Come on. That was never raised that as a campaign issue. We have no real opposition party in this town. The real estate collapse drove people's home prices down to levels no one could imagine a few years ago."

"Everyone faces that problem," he said.

"Yes," she countered. "But a family's home is its most valued possession, and not just financially. Now that value has disappeared. Foreclosures in town are at an all time high."

"I know that. These are tough times to be a mayor. Cuts have to be made. What would you do instead?"

Rosie Ravioli was well prepared. "You are proposing we shrink not only public worker benefits, but now you are cutting public employees as well. These people and their unions are what made Menlo Grove. Laying off more people will only make the economy in town worse. No job, no salary, no way to pay the mortgage, buy groceries, eat in a restaurant. We cannot lose the support of our public sector workers."

Mayor Kim realized the triumvirate of the police, fire, and teacher unions saw an opening to get the much more labor friendly, and some would say, pliable, Rosie Ravioli in office. She clearly was more than willing to play their game.

"Give me twenty-four hours," Kim said. "Let's meet again tomorrow."

"That will be fine, Mr. Mayor. See you tonight?"

"Tonight?" Mayor Kim asked innocently.

"Yes, at the Menlo Grove Gourmet, of course," she said quickly as she and her band exited the room.

The Menlo Grove Gourmet began as a fund-raiser for numerous charities in town. Obviously, being new to Menlo Grove, Assistant Superintendent Michael Ferrone had never attended or even heard of the Menlo Grove Gourmet. DelVecchio had called Ferrone to his office the day before the event.

"Tomorrow is the Menlo Grove Gourmet. We are expected to attend."

"The Menlo Grove Gourmet?" Ferrone asked.

"Local restaurants buy table space at Grove Manor, the big banquet hall in town. Every restaurant will have samples of its food. All kinds of ethnic food available. Doesn't cost much for a ticket."

"Sounds like a nice community affair," Ferrone said.

"It begins at 7:00 P.M."

"Another fifteen-hour day," Ferrone muttered.

"Whatever," DelVecchio replied. "Thank you."

When Ferrone arrived at the event after work, he could see every would-be politician in both the town and the county making an appearance. Local newspapers, radio, and television stations had sent reporters. Food plus politicians equaled media. Even the Board of Education members were present.

The mixture of aromas from the food filled the great ballroom. The first person Ferrone saw when he entered the large ballroom was the very cute and very friendly Board of Education member Debbie Duhan. Duhan smiled as she approached Ferrone, took his face in both her hands and kissed him flush on the lips.

"So happy you could attend, Mr. Ferrone," she said. "You will see all that Menlo Grove has to offer here tonight."

When she kissed him, Ferrone had taken a half step backward, thinking to himself, "In all my years in education, I don't think I've ever been kissed by a Board member before. Certainly not on the lips."

"So glad I could be here," Ferrone responded, wondering if his $50 entry ticket was tax deductible, seeing that he was still wearing the navy blue suit he had put on thirteen hours ago.

"Wonder what she means by 'all Menlo Grove has to offer?'" he thought.

His eyes wandered the room searching for familiar faces. Duhan took him by the arm. "I want you to meet someone," she said.

Ferrone saw DelVecchio munching on a spare rib and talking to Board vice president Vito Viterelli. Next to DelVecchio, his wife, Concetta, smiled and made small talk with Board president Bill Burton. She clutched a glass of white wine and nibbled on something small.

"Oh, there's Larry Griffiths. He is on my curriculum committee," Ferrone said, pointing to the older man in tweed. "I'd like to say hello."

"No, Mr. Ferrone, Larry is sitting with that Aashiyani Gupta. Rumor has it that she will be running in the next Board election against me. Gupta is saying the Board should have never put up for a vote another building referendum after the last six were all defeated. You don't want to be seen with that group. We don't sit next to them," she directed.

"Oh, okay," Ferrone agreed.

He thought to himself, "This is like a kid moving to a new middle school. Who can talk to whom. Where it is okay for the new kid to sit and whom the new kid must avoid."

"You know," she began, "the union supported me on my first run for the Board. However, I voted against the 'leave of absence' for former superintendent Clair Smith. The union did not support me in the next election. I won anyway."

"You don't need the union," Ferrone smiled at her.

"Oh, you are very sweet," she giggled. "But it's easier when they are on your side," Duhan admitted. "They know I always support the teachers. And I will never vote against anything that helps the special ed kids."

The lines between the pro-DelVecchio/anti-Mayor Kim Board members and the anti-DelVecchio/pro-Mayor Kim members were clearly drawn. Ferrone knew he needed to identify those lines and know when to cross and when to avoid.

All those years of teaching pronoun agreement and coaching how to defense a bunt had not prepared him for this game. There were clearly new lessons to be learned.

Duhan continued to lead Ferrone through the crowd while holding his left arm tightly against her right breast. They stopped at a large round table filled with people Ferrone did not know. Debbie did the introductions.

"I would like to introduce everyone to Michael Ferrone. He is our new Assistant Superintendent for Curriculum and Instruction."

A short, rather stout woman stood up and shook Ferrone's hand. "Happy to meet you, Mr. Ferrone. I am Rosie Ravioli, member of the town council."

"Nice to meet you, too, Ms. Ravioli. Nice to meet everyone," Ferrone said, glancing over Ravioli's head to the others at the table behind her. The people around the table offered polite hellos or raised the glass of their beverage of choice.

"Hope you can get those test scores up," Rosie Ravioli said. "We have a great school system here in Menlo Grove. I went to elementary and high school with Superintendent DelVecchio. He was so handsome and such a great athlete. Everyone had such a crush on him."

"Acting Superintendent," Debbie Duhan politely reminded the soon to be announced primary challenger to the mayor. Duhan was a DelVecchio ally now, but she liked to play it down the middle. And she really did care about kids.

Ferrone just smiled. His head began to hurt.

Throughout the evening, Ferrone met, conversed, and did his own share of munching and drinking. Drinking in extreme moderation, of course.

DelVecchio always reminded his people. "The public holds us to a higher standard. They expect us to be saints. Be careful what you do in public." A philosophy Ferrone had embraced long before meeting DelVecchio.

Mayor Kim and his group of supporters sat on one side of the room; intra-party challenger Rosie Ravioli and her group sat on the other. Pro-DelVecchio Board members spoke during the night with Ravioli's group. The anti-DelVecchio people spoke only to those at Mayor Kim's table.

However, during the evening Mayor Kim began to realize that those who voted against the building referendum were not necessarily his supporters either. Apparently, many people voted no on the school referendum vote because the automatic no voters had come out in much greater numbers than usual for a school vote in December.

Union Boss Kristoff Kaifes and his assistants had a table of their own. Different people from both sides stopped by to pay their respects. DelVecchio made several visits, as did several Board of Ed members. The police and fire people each had their own areas of the room. From these tables Ferrone recognized only Board member and police deputy chief Tony Martino.

Martino was a big supporter of DelVecchio, however, because Martino's wife worked in the school district, he was unable to cast a vote on many issues, including DelVecchio's new contract.

As far as DelVecchio was concerned, Martino served as a good contact with the police union, but he was a waste of a Board member since he couldn't vote on so many issues. And especially because he could not count as one of the five votes DelVecchio needed for his new contract approval.

DelVecchio and Board president Burton had been in hiding since the school building referendum came crashing down all around them two nights ago. Even though they had hoped for the best and expected the worse, the devastating margin of the defeat could not be sugarcoated.

"Our main goal now is to get you a new contract," Burton stated. "But we have to be certain we have the five votes."

"I have the five votes," DelVecchio stated clearly.

Burton turned on his analytic lawyerly tone. "The defeat of the referendum tells me there are a lot of people out there willing to come out and vote against whatever we are selling. Not every one of your supporters on the Board may remain loyal to you if they need to appease the naysayers to get re-elected."

"We'll do what we need to do to get the five votes," DelVecchio said.

Despite the turmoil he had helped cause by working silently to defeat the school referendum, Mayor Kim knew he had his own problems. He had talked to many people tonight about the defeat of the school referendum. But what he had confirmed was those who voted against the school were not supporting his office either. He had angered the local unions big time. And the anti-union people in town seemed to be in the mood to vote against anything and everything.

By the end of the night of glad-handing, eating, drinking, and politicking, Mayor Kim realized he could not win a primary challenge. Rosie Ravioli and her group had far more supporters who would show up to vote in a primary than he. The backup quarterback of a struggling football team is always the most popular guy in town. And Rosie right now was playing the role of the backup. The die was cast. Kim decided he would cancel tomorrow's meeting with Ravioli and her group.

Instead, he would hold a press conference announcing his decision not to run for re-election as mayor so he could spend more time with his family.

SIXTEEN

THE UNION BOSS

Kristott Kaifes, president of the Menlo Grove Teachers' Association, never missed attending the annual Menlo Grove Gourmet. This event afforded a perfect opportunity to touch base with every political faction in town. Not to mention allowing everyone to observe who was kanoodling with whom.

Kaifes arrived at the event thirty minutes early to get a good table with enough chairs for his assistants, and the building representatives who might attend. Past association officers often attended to visit old friends and foes.

The teachers' union always managed to secure its own centrally located table at the event - a place located so those at the table could see every person as he or she entered the large ballroom.

Kaifes was already finished making his second trip around the tables of many local restaurants that had rented space and were offering samples of their delicacies for a minimal cost. He was savoring teriyaki chicken and sipping his third whiskey on the rocks when he spotted Board of Education member Debbie Duhan entering.

Duhan looked stunning in the yellow blouse, pale blue jacket and skirt that she wore highlighting her blue eyes and blond hair. Though she smoked and drank for many years, she still possessed an attractive figure.

Although the union did not support Duhan in the last Board election, Kaifes was well aware that she was an important ally. She always supported special educa-tion, and this division always offered great opportunities to increase the number of special education teachers, aides, paraprofessionals, and secretarial staff. All of these employees added to the rolls of the rank and file members of the union.

Although Kaifes preferred for people to come to him, for Duhan, he walked from his table toward her.

"Good evening, Debbie," Kaifes greeted her, bending to kiss her on the cheek and holding her just a moment lon-ger than appropriate, long enough for his forearm to brush the front of her jacket.

"You get better looking every time I see you," he said.

"And you get drunker every time I see you," Duhan replied.

"Aw, come on, Deb. Are you still angry with me? That was a couple of elections ago," Kaifes cooed in his smarmi-est, bedroom voice.

"I won without you," Duhan stated proudly. "And you weren't much help on getting the building referendum passed."

"The Governor is making noise about cutting state aid, Deb. He'll be looking for the district to cut Menlo Grove's well respected special services we offer to children," Kaifes said, ignoring Duhan's pronouncement. "You know what we offer in special ed is second to none."

"We won't be making any cuts in special ed, not as long as I sit on this Board," she clearly replied.

"Let's make up then, Deb. We can work together."

Duhan was no longer paying attention to Kaifes. She noticed that Michael Ferrone, the new Assistant Superintendent of Curriculum and Instruction, had just entered the room.

"Bye, doll," she said smiling and glancing back momentarily at the union boss, completely ignoring Kaifes's offer of open arms and another grope. She had turned away and now headed directly in Ferrone's direction.

Acting Superintendent Michael DelVecchio approached Kaifes glumly as the association president watched Duhan saunter away.

"Kristoff, we need to talk," DelVecchio said without any opening greeting.

"About the referendum?" Kristoff asked.

"No," DelVecchio answered with and angry wave of his hand. "That's history."

"What's up, Mike?" Kristoff asked.

"We've got budget issues," DelVecchio declared.

"Mike, what else is new? When haven't we had budget issues?" Kristoff asked with nonchalance.

"No," DelVecchio corrected him, "this is serious. Our state funding has been cut big time, and I need to find major bucks in next year's budget."

"What do you have in mind?" Kristoff asked.

"If I can go from full-day to half-day kindergarten, I can save over three million bucks."

"Now, Mike, you know I can't agree to that. You cut back to half-day kindergarten, that means you'll only need half the number of kindergarten teachers."

"How else can I save money? I'm spending 80 cents of every dollar on personnel. It's my biggest expense," DelVecchio stated calmly.

"Personnel is not an expense," rebutted Kaifes just as calmly. "Teachers are human capital. I prefer to see workers as an asset, not a debit."

"Save it for your union meetings. I need to find four million dollars. You need to help me get a big piece of that."

"The association will help in any way we can, but I cannot support cutting kindergarten," Kaifes declared conclusively.

"You don't have to support it. Stop by tomorrow morning at 10:00, I'll show you the numbers," DelVecchio said and he walked away.

The next morning at 10:20, Kaifes strolled casually into DelVecchio's office as the acting superintendent was closing his cell phone.

Kaifes began the conversation. "The mayor is going to announce he is not running for re-election."

"I'm well aware of that," DelVecchio said.

"Rosie will run?" Kaifes inquired.

"That's right," DelVecchio replied. "She will be much better for us. She'll work more closely with us."

"How?"

"She says the town owns a vacant building they could sell to us for $1.00, and we could renovate it to use as a school. This town will never approve a building referendum in this economy," DelVecchio replied.

"How much to renovate, and where will you get the money for that?" Kaifes asked.

"We'll find the money," DelVecchio declared in an even tone.

"Then maybe you won't need to cut full-day kindergarten," Kaifes smiled mischievously. "Let's talk about this tenure case you're pushing," Kaifes said, changing the subject.

"Kristoff, this teacher did not show up for her supplemental instruction classes, and when she did show up, sometimes she gave the kids worksheets to do which she never scored or even looked at, and at other times she gave them free time to read."

"Nothing wrong with free reading time," Kaifes stated.

"Shit, the kids weren't reading at all; they were playing cards," retorted DelVecchio.

"You got all of this documented?" Kaifes asked.

"We have enough," DelVecchio replied.

"If it's not ALL documented, I wouldn't want to bet you have nearly enough," retorted the Union Boss. "The arbiter will have to decide."

"That's so expensive," DelVecchio declared. "We've already spent several hundred thousand dollars in legal fees and lost work time for her administrators and supervisor to give depositions and testimony. You know all this."

"Yes, it's called due process," said Kaifes.

"It's got to be easier to get rid of an incompetent teacher," DelVecchio claimed.

"Well, until it is, her local association and the state association will defend her as we would any teacher."

"I know that," DelVecchio said. "But Lilly has missed so much time on this case, and now she's retiring, and Lucy, the elementary supervisor, had gotten virtually nothing else done while gathering documentation on the teacher's incompetence. Same goes for the teacher's principal."

"You mean principals," Kaifes corrected DelVecchio.

Both men knew the teacher had been transferred from building to building, like a rotten hot potato, with the hope the district could keep her one step ahead of the complaints from the parents.

In truth, most people would agree that the teacher should have never been given tenure in the first place, however when she first became a teacher supervision of instruction was in the dark ages. Very little accountability was part of the process back then.

The general rule of thumb for bad teachers was "Keep the students quiet and in your room."

Unruly students and incompetent teachers had an agreement. "You stay quiet and don't make a ruckus, and I won't give you work to do."

State testing had changed all that. And now getting rid of an incompetent teacher would cost money. Lots of money.

"Ah, we'll figure it out," DelVecchio said with a wave of his hand. Maybe you can get her to retire."

"I hear she'll go on disability for a while, but we'll see," Kaifes replied. "I'll talk to you later at lunch."

With that the president of the teachers' association left the Acting Superintendent's office and walked down the long hallway. Michael Ferrone, Assistant Superintendent for

Curriculum and Instruction, almost immediately intercepted him.

"Kristoff, come in. I want to run something by you," said the new guy.

"Hey," Kristoff answered, "the new guy. How's it going?"

Kristoff entered Ferrone's office, took three pieces of chocolate from Ferrone's candy dish, and sat down.

"Kristoff, do you realize teachers in Menlo Grove don't get their lesson plans checked?" Ferrone asked.

"Not true," Kaifes answered, "lesson plans are checked when a teacher is observed."

Ferrone was prepared for this. "I've read those observations. About half of the reports don't mention whether the lesson plans were available for review or not."

"Then that's the supervisor's or principal's fault," Kaifes replied.

"Not the point," answered Ferrone. "I've worked in several districts around the state. Every district requires lesson plans be reviewed weekly. You guys do it once a year? Come on."

"Once a year for tenured teachers. Three times a year if you're non-tenured."

"That's ridiculous, Kristoff."

"It's in the contract," Kaifes said proudly.

"You're still missing the point. The monitoring guidelines state that lesson plans must be reviewed at least monthly." Ferrone opened the state-monitoring book to show Kaifes the text explaining exactly what Ferrone had just stated.

"Menlo Grove is a high performing district even without lesson plans."

"Well, if we don't change the current practice, the state won't consider us high performing, and it will be in all the newspapers," Ferrone stated. "Parents will be all over DelVecchio, and the Board will have to answer for it. The state says we must check lesson plans regularly or we fail monitoring."

"I never knew that," Kaifes said.

"Obviously, neither did the Board representatives who negotiated that teachers' contract," Ferrone replied.

"What do you propose?" Kaifes seemed anxious at the prospect of negotiation.

"I've already met with the principals and the supervisors separately," Ferrone stated.

"Yes, I heard about that," said Kaifes.

"We've drawn up a proposal for lesson plan review. The language follows the state monitoring guidelines verbatim. We'll have the teachers send their plans electronically to their supervisor. We'll archive the plans up here so they'll be available for the state monitors."

"Good luck. First of all, the district doesn't have the technology to handle that," Kaifes stated truthfully.

"The district has no money for anything but paying teachers to stay after school to provide extra help for kids and paying you to walk around buildings unannounced," Ferrone said with a smile on his face.

"And second, you can't keep plans on file," Kaifes stated.

"Why can't we keep plans on file?" asked Ferrone.

"Plans belong to the teacher," said Kaifes.

"Not according to case law," Ferrone pulled out another document and showed Kaifes a highlighted passage.

"Work completed as part of employment is considered the property of the employer."

"It's called 'Work For Hire.'"

Kaifes blinked as he read the passage, "Give me a copy of that and your proposal. I'll talk to my people."

"Good. When can we meet again?" Ferrone asked.

"Call my secretary. She knows my schedule better than I do."

"I cannot believe you have a full time secretary," Ferrone said.

"It's a big district, my friend," Kaifes stated, and grabbing two more chocolates, he disappeared quickly out the door and down the hallway.

SEVENTEEN

THE PRINCIPALS

The morning after the school referendum had been overwhelmingly rejected, a very groggy Assistant Superintendent for Curriculum and Instruction Michael Ferrone sat at his desk at 7:10 A.M. He busily collected district, state code, and monitoring policies on lesson plans for about forty minutes when his phone rang.

"Good morning, Michael Ferrone."

"Hi, Michael, this is Cyndi Zubricki. How are you?" The elementary principal cooed into the phone.

"Oh, Hi Cyndi, I'm fine. Late night last night. Not a good result."

"Yes, that's why I'm calling you this morning," Zubricki said.

Ferrone, somewhat bewildered that one of the three she-wolves had called him rather than Acting Superintendent DelVecchio, replied coolly, "Yes, it was awful. We got killed. I'm sorry, Cyndi, but you won't be getting your building expansion."

"I figured as much. The parents don't seem to mind that I have to cram their kids into the same dark, little area for gym, for lunches, and for assemblies. Don't know how I'll do next year's schedule. I need to add a fourth lunch period, so I don't know where I can move the gym classes."

"Rosemary has her kids eat in their classrooms," Ferrone offered.

"I've been trying to avoid that. The kids are sitting in the same place virtually all day now. That would mean they couldn't even leave their room for lunch."

"It stinks, I know," Ferrone said.

"I called you because I am afraid of DelVecchio's mood today," Zubricki explained.

"Yes, he will be a bear today."

"Does he have a backup plan now that the referendum has been defeated?" Zubricki asked.

"Not that I know of. Seven referendums in a row have failed. And the budget numbers for next year don't look good."

"Well, we'll discuss our ideas at our monthly principals' luncheon," she said. "I was just wondering if you had any clue as to his plans for the next step."

"He told us that he would keep offering referendums until he got one passed," Ferrone offered.

"But they keep getting shot down by bigger numbers."

"I know, Cyndi, but I really have nothing else to tell you," Ferrone explained. "Since you called, could I ask you if you have completed your school-level plan? I haven't seen it yet. It was due to this office last Friday."

"Yes, I know. I'm almost finished with it. I had three band parents here yesterday to complain about the cost of renting instruments, a Board member stop by unannounced, two teachers in a spat I had to mediate, a nine year old boy who won't stop pinching the girls, and an eleven year old girl who came to school dressed like Lady GaGa."

"Okay, get it in as soon as possible. I need your numbers for a state report," Ferrone calmly replied. "Thanks, Cyndi."

As Ferrone hung up the phone, he rubbed his eyes. Being a principal was a job he never wanted, and he admired those who successfully completed this impossible task every day.

He needed to review the Menlo Park South High School numbers again. Principal Applegate looked to be in deep trouble with the Board of Ed, and therefore, with Acting Superintendent DelVecchio. However, the more he looked, the more Ferrone found that the "troubled" high school in the southern part of town was doing fine, especially considering the difficult demographic attending the place.

Calling an entire building of two thousand students a "failing school" because one small subgroup of thirty special education students had failed to meet a benchmark seemed ridiculous on its face. The vast majority of students in the building had done very well on the state tests.

The phone rang again.

"Michael, this is Rosemarie."

"Good morning, Rosemarie. How are you this morning?"

"Pissed," answered Rosemarie Grogan-Unangst, elementary principal and the second third of the three she-wolves, as well as president of the town council.

Ferrone wondered what was going on. First a call from Zubricki, now one from Grogan-Unangst. There was big concern on the principals' part about another failed referendum. They were running their programs in little, very old, and deteriorating spaces.

"Yes, we are all disappointed that the referendum went down to defeat again," Ferrone began. "Mr. DelVecchio is not in a good mood," he added, anticipating her next question.

"That's just the start of it," Grogan-Unangst interrupted. "There is talk that the Mayor may face a primary challenge. I think it may have been a mistake to get involved in town politics."

She was a big supporter of the Mayor Kim, and if he were to be replaced as mayor, the new mayor's allies on the council would soon see to it that Rosemarie was replaced as council president.

"No, Rosemarie, you are good. But will you resign if Mayor Kim is replaced?" Ferrone asked.

"I haven't decided," she answered hesitantly.

Ferrone knew that she was being somewhat disingenuous. As these local political wars played out, an ousted mayor's allies on the town council often resigned when the mayor left office.

"But the real reason I called you today concerns my test scores," Grogan-Unangst continued.

"I know they went down some," Ferrone said. "I wouldn't be overly concerned, Rosemarie, your scores are still okay."

"Not good enough," she added. "I need to keep my English Language Learners passing at the higher benchmark this year. If they don't, my entire school looks like it's failing, according to the state. It's not fair!"

As standardized test scores rose in importance in measuring a school's success, principals had become obsessed with worry over every increasing benchmarks for passing rates across all the subgroups.

She was not finished. "Getting students who are just learning English as their second language to pass at these higher percentages is becoming just impossible."

Ferrone interjected, "And it is also getting very expensive with all the supplemental instruction we have to give them to get them up to speed. Rosemarie, I don't know where we are going to get the money for this next year."

"How about the Christmas tree money we got from the state senator last year?"

"I am really getting tired of this Christmas tree money talk," Ferrone replied. "There is no more Christmas tree money. That may have been a pork-filled political payoff of some sort. The money is gone. Our job is to raise the test scores of our students."

"I know this is not about testing the students," she protested.

"What do you think it's about?" Ferrone asked.

"This is all about testing the educators," she declared.

This small change of emphasis had made a dramatic change in the relationship between principals and teachers.

"I don't like to get yelled and screamed at by the Superintendent because my school did not keep up with the ever-increasing benchmarks," Rosemarie angrily spat out the words. "And I don't like to yell and scream at my teachers for the same reason. My teachers work very hard."

"Rosemarie, no one said your teachers aren't working hard," Ferrone tried to mediate Rosemarie as she continued having an argument with herself.

"This is not good for building morale. Our public schools in Menlo Grove have a long history of success," she said. "Why do some of these politicians want to prove all public schools are failures?"

"We need to get every one of our elementary schools in the district following the same curriculum and best practice," Ferrone offered.

"Oh, I know where you're going," Grogan-Unangst interjected. "You think Lucy Williams knows it all."

"It doesn't matter what I think," Ferrone answered. "She is the curriculum expert, the elementary supervisor, and she has put together a curriculum that works. Too many principals think they have their own answers. This district's elementary schools have been permitted to do their own thing for too long, Rosemarie, and that has hurt every school."

"Every school in Menlo Grove is different. You haven't seemed to learn this yet. Mr. DelVecchio has given us enough space to do what we know is best for our own neighborhood," she said.

"Doesn't seem to be working," Ferrone rebutted.

"Good bye," she said abruptly.

Despite the fact that he didn't trust her, Ferrone clearly liked Grogan-Unangst, and they had an amiable relationship. He was also clearly getting the idea that in order to keep political peace by giving his favorite principals so much leeway, DelVecchio had mismanaged the overall district. The standardized test results were a big worry and a constant complaint of educators, but the scores were like those of a ballgame from when Ferrone was a coach.

Once someone in power begins keeping score, you just can't hide from the numbers. The numbers are all that matter.

EIGHTEEN

THE BOARD OF ED

The December Board meeting was shorter than usual, and held earlier in the month, due to the holidays. The closed session meeting, however, held following the public portion, often lasted longer, because as the mid-year approached, issues began to accumulate.

Test scores began being released to the public, principals started to look at non-renewing or transferring staff, and the special education lawsuits continued rolling in. In addition, the defeat of the school building referendum proved a blow to every Board member. All the members knew the district school buildings were both outdated and overcrowded.

During the twenty-minute break between the public and closed sessions, a few people, including DelVecchio and

Debbie Duhan, took a cigarette break behind the building, several ran to the restrooms, and all snapped up a plate and utensils to grab a late dinner from the buffet table set up in a conference room.

"Wow, this is nice," Ferrone said to Lilly Laboy at the first Board meeting he had attended. "I thought we weren't permitted to use public funds for food anymore," he said to Lilly in a questioning tone.

"The public doesn't pay for this," she replied. "Our food service provider provides this food to us gratis."

"You're kidding?" Ferrone asked rhetorically. "We purchase their services, and in return they supply us with a free meal every month?"

"Don't worry about it. No one else does," she answered.

Ferrone let it go. The food was delicious.

Board president Bill Burton opened the closed session portion as most of the other Board members, Acting Superintendent DelVecchio, and Board attorney Bob Butterfield munched on chicken marsala, tilapia oreganata, grilled vegetables, and baked potatoes. Business administrator Dan Maris spooned from a cup of lobster bisque. It helped settle his fiery stomach. Ferrone finished a large brownie with walnuts while sipping a fresh cup of coffee. Laboy nibbled strawberries.

"Our first item," Burton began, "is a new nepotism policy the state demands every Board of Education ratify."

"Wait a minute," vice president Vito Viterelli interrupted. "I never got reimbursed for driving to the School Boards Association Convention."

Burton looked at Viterelli in askance. "We got free hotel rooms for three nights, all paid for from the district budget; our health provider, law firm, and copier companies bought our dinners each night; and various other corporations provided us with free food and drink all day every day at their receptions. And you're complaining about not being reimbursed for mileage?"

"I only want what I legally deserve," Viterelli whined.

Burton looked at DelVecchio.

"I'll talk to the secretary and get it done tomorrow," the Acting Superintendent declared.

"And by the way, Dan," Burton said to Dan Maris, the Business Administrator, "how did you get the copier company to pay for dinner for all of us and our spouses?"

Dan grinned widely, "It was part of our agreement with the copier company when we agreed to change from the old outfit. Unwritten agreement, of course. We got better copiers, a lower monthly rental, and a free meal, with drinks, for forty people."

"What are we paying to lease copiers?" Board member Debbie Duhan asked.

"About fifty grand a month," Dan answered without hesitation.

"Whoo," Debbie responded.

"That meal was great, though," DelVecchio joked as most of the room broke up with laughter.

Board member Larry Griffiths, again dressed in tweed blazer, was not smiling, and tried to get the conversation back on track. "What is this nepotism policy the state demands we ratify?"

Board president Burton looked at DelVecchio who looked at Ferrone. Ferrone was in charge of keeping track of policy, and the state's Department of Education regularly sent him email updates with Board policies that had to be revised.

Ferrone was prepared for this question. His last policy sub-committee meeting with four members of the Board had reviewed the new nepotism mandate just two nights earlier at their meeting. "The state has provided a list of people, specifically Board members and the superintendent, who cannot hire anyone related to them. They have also included a definition of who is considered a relative."

Daniel Wells, retired teacher and former supervisor who now sat on the Board, raised his voice in protest. "That's not right," he began. "This is an insult to all of us. The state has no business telling us who to hire. They are insinuating that the members of this Board would hire a relative instead of the best available candidate."

Wells' wife and both his sons were employees of the district.

"I agree with you," Vito Viterelli said, dribbling marsala sauce from his chin as he spoke. "It's an insult."

Larry Griffiths looked annoyed. "Just a minute, just a minute. Let me make my point," he said.

Board president Burton kept order. "Let Larry make his point," Burton demanded.

Griffiths looked around the room. "I am not insulted by the nepotism law," the older man began. "I do not believe any Board should even think about hiring a relative. What bothers me is the state is doing our job for us. They are telling us what policy to ratify, and even what that policy must include. What happened to local control?'

"Yeah," Viterelli agreed again.

"What are our options?" Burton asked counselor Butterfield, who seemed more involved with a chocolate chip cookie than he was with the issue at hand.

Butterfield looked up. "Mr. Ferrone, would you summarize what the state is saying the Board must do?"

Ferrone tried to speak, but was interrupted by Burton. "The state says we must adopt a nepotism policy, and the state is telling us what must be in that policy."

Butterfield smiled slightly. "Then the Board has to adopt that policy." He looked at Ferrone. "What are the consequences if the Board does not adopt said policy?"

Ferrone looked down at his notes, "Loss of state aid."

Nearly everyone in the room groaned. The amount of state aid Menlo Grove had been receiving had been diminishing annually for a decade, despite the increasing number of students.

"I say we don't adopt it," Viterelli proposed.

"Wait a minute," said Daniel Wells, suddenly the voice of reason. "We can't do that. What if we adopted the policy but added a protest statement and sent it back to the state?"

All eyes moved to counsel. Butterfield shrugged his shoulders. "That would be fine," he said. "Sounds like the state only cares that you adopt the policy. You can add a protest statement if you like."

Larry Griffiths raised his hand to speak again. "I have another question," he began. "This conversation we're having appears to be about policy. Why are we having it in closed session? I thought closed session topics were limited to personnel. This doesn't seem right."

Butterfield didn't hesitate this time. "He's right. Policy is for public session. As your legal counsel, I would advise Board president Burton to change the subject."

"Okay. Next topic," Burton pronounced.

Board member and high school science teacher Carla Casella raised her hand to speak. "Can we discuss the referendum? What is the Board's plan now that another one has gone down to defeat?"

DelVecchio spoke up, "The Board has decided to put up another building referendum in the spring."

"When did the Board decide that?" Larry Griffiths asked in wonderment.

DelVecchio's eyes shifted to the left. Burton jumped in, "I have spoken to Mr. DelVecchio and a few other Board members about our plan."

"I wasn't invited to this meeting," Griffiths protested.

"Neither was I," added Suzee Semanski, Griffiths' partner in anti-DelVecchio sentiment.

"Well," Burton explained, "it was part of a Buildings and Grounds meeting."

"But you're not a member of that committee," declared Griffiths.

"I am," protested Semanski. "I don't remember discussing the referendum at our meeting."

"Well, it was a sub-committee meeting. And although I am not officially a member of the committee, the Board president is a member of every committee, if he so wishes," Burton declared.

"Why are we talking about this?" Burton continued, realizing he needed to change the subject. "The referendum isn't personnel; I don't think we should be discussing this in closed session.' He looked at Butterfield. "Should we, Bill?"

"No," Butterfield answered, suppressing a burp.

"Good, let's move on," Burton said. "We have three issues to discuss. First, the union and some members of the public are not happy that we have hired a teacher as Lilly's replacement for Assistant Superintendent of Student

Services. Also, some people have written in the blogs that we hired Lilly's replacement because our candidate fits a racial "profile."

"Should I leave?" Lilly asked. She was attending her final Board meeting before retiring. The public portion of the Board meeting had been filled with accolades from Board members and some members of the public for her service to the district. Ironically, she felt uncomfortable being in the closed session as the Board discussed her replacement even though she chaired the interview committee.

"No, stay," DelVecchio said to her

"I'm just saying," Burton offered. "Be aware that to some people it's an issue. Three of you are running for re-election in the spring. Opponents are going to use this issue."

"What has this to do with personnel? You are talking about candidates for the next Board election!" Larry Griffiths practically rose out of his seat.

Burton looked at counselor Butterfield again. Butterfield shrugged his shoulders again.

"Okay, issue number two," Burton continued. The recently released test scores have placed Menlo Grove South High School once again in the category of ' School in Need of Improvement.' We need to offer students school choice to Henry Ford High School because of this."

"Oh, my God," Debbie Duhan interjected. "What does that mean?"

"It means we have a potential nightmare on our hands," Burton answered.

"I'll tell you what it means," Vito Viterelli had again taken the floor. "It means we have to get rid of that principal. That Applegarth guy."

"Applegate," DelVecchio corrected him. "The personnel committee has already discussed this issue. I am in charge of that committee, though Lilly runs it for me, and the people sitting in this room who are on that committee have discussed the possibility of replacing Mr. Applegate as principal of Menlo Grove South High School."

"The public is demanding we do something. We must give them something before the Board election in the spring," Viterelli said.

"Are we talking about elections again?" Griffiths had lost his patience. "Do we have to frame every issue around elections?"

"Hey, I don't care," said Viterelli, "I'm not up for re-election this time."

"Okay," Burton broke in. "The Personnel committee will discuss Mr. Applegate's renewal or non-renewal based on Mr. DelVecchio's evaluation of him, and we will discuss that at our next meeting."

Board president Burton doggedly continued. "The third issue is the tenure charges we have brought against the special ed teacher. This has dragged on now for a year and at great expense to the Board. Bill, how is the court case going?"

Counselor Butterfield opened his notes. "We've had two of her principals, her supervisor, and Lilly get cross-examined the past two weeks."

"How does our case look?" Burton inquired.

"The Board has a solid case," Butterfield said. "But some of our witnesses are not that strong. They're teachers by nature, background, and experience. They are always trying to see both sides."

Lilly looked at the ceiling. "That's who they are."

"Not when they're on the stand testifying," DelVecchio said.

"The Board should win the case. But it is going to take a lot longer. The teacher has her own witnesses yet to testify."

"How much longer?" Burton asked.

Butterfield shrugged his shoulders and reached for another cookie.

PART 3

THIRD MARKING PERIOD

NINETEEN

THE SUPERVISOR

The failure of the building referendum, like Board elections themselves, had no immediate impact on any of the ten curriculum supervisors in the district. This group focused on two central issues: aligning each course or grade level curriculum to that of the core content standards, from which the state testing was developed; and providing the training, classroom observation, and evaluation of teachers.

Scott Perrillo served as principal of the school building where Lucy Williams had arrived for a 4:00 principals' and supervisors' association meeting. Lucy met a middle-aged teacher leaving the rest room and wiping her eyes on her handkerchief. The halls were empty of children, but some teachers remained in their classrooms wrapping up business for the day and getting a head start on tomorrow's lessons.

"Is everything okay?" Lucy asked.

"Oh, I'm fine," Judy Blinkley responded. Then added bitterly, "but I cannot be expected to teach next to THAT woman!"

It was common knowledge in the district that Judy's ex-husband, Ron Blinkley, who had taught in the same building, had divorced Judy and married Sharon Johansson, a somewhat younger and prettier teacher, who also taught in the same building as the Ron and Judy Blinkley. The affair had been going on for two years before Mr. Blinkley announced to Judy that he wanted a divorce. Judy, already embarrassed beyond words about the affair, granted the divorce but kept the surname because of her two children with Ron.

Now the second Mrs. Blinkley had been moved to a classroom adjacent to the first Mrs. Blinkley. The two Mrs. Blinkleys were teaching in classrooms next to one another. The staff called that hallway the Blinkley wing of the building. The singular Mr. Blinkley had asked to be transferred to a school across town.

Lucy placed her arm around Judy's shoulder. Everyone had marriage issues, but one had to admit, Judy Blinkley's were unique, even for Menlo Grove.

"You're a strong person, Judy," Lucy said calmly. "I will talk to the principal about getting your room changed."

"I've been in that classroom for twenty years. I shouldn't have to move because of HER. Let her move." Judy's eyes rose toward the sky, "That bitch!"

"I've got to get to a meeting. Sorry, " Lucy explained, patting Judy on the shoulder. "You hang in there."

Judy Blinkley may not have been the best teacher in the district, or even in her building, but no one deserved to have to deal with having the new wife of one's ex-husband teaching in the next classroom. Not only that, but Judy's ex-husband had recently been awarded the teacher of the year in the building at the conclusion of his final year there. Lucy never felt more frustration than when such a teacher would be honored annually as Teacher of the Year, selected by a committee consisting of several stakeholders, including main office administrators, other teachers and parents. But no supervisor.

Lucy had observed Mr. Blinkley and knew he was nowhere near the top half of teachers in his building. She had been the only one to observe this teacher actually teach. He had been long tenured and had recently announced his transfer across town. He was not in the same league as the many outstanding and younger educators she had seen during the year. Apparently they had to wait their turn. No one had asked the supervisor.

When Lucy entered the little room used as a miniature library where the after school meeting would be held, about half of the principals and supervisors were already crowded into the small space and were chatting. A few would arrive shortly, but most of the remaining administrators would not attend the meeting, as they were still busy stamping out brushfires that had erupted in their buildings at dismissal time.

The Principals' and Supervisors' Association president and elementary principal Scott Perrillo began to speak. "The Board wants to put us on merit pay for our next contract. They refuse to begin negotiations until we agree to make merit pay part of our language."

Immediately, a disgruntled growl rose from those in the room.

"The Board wants to pay us on merit, and not the teachers?" screeched Barbara Jean Cox, elementary principal and she-wolf.

Scott continued, "The Board wants to try out the idea of merit pay on a smaller scale before it moves toward trying to add it to the teachers' contract," he said in an even voice.

"Scott, the teachers are not going to go for that," shouted Cyndi Zubricki, another elementary principal and she-wolf.

"It might not matter," Scott said. "The state may put merit pay in every educator's contract language. The Board wants to experiment with a smaller negotiating unit if and when that happens."

"Bullshit," shouted middle school principal Lou Ferrigno.

"Just a minute. Just a minute," Scott interjected. "Hear me out. I did some figuring."

Bobby Jones, supervisor of P.E. and Health, and former coaching colleague when both worked at Menlo Grove South High School, smiled and shouted, "Uh, oh. Scott did some figuring. Now we're in trouble."

Scott Perrillo was nothing if not determined. He had done some figuring, and was about to explain what he had figured to his seemingly closed-minded colleagues.

"The Board agreed we could be part of writing the guidelines for measuring our effectiveness as administrators and supervisors," Scott explained.

"Will test scores be included in these *guidelines*?" high school guidance supervisor Jill Hillebrand asked.

"Yes, of course," Scott continued, "but this will allow us to implement the cross-curricular reform all of us have wanted our teachers to do."

"How?" Jill asked.

"Because we will include scores in our evaluations, and the only tests the state gives right now are in Language

Arts, Math, and Science, we will now be able to implement reading, writing, and math across the curriculum."

"I'm still confused," Cyndi Zubricki yelled from her seat in the back of the room.

"Let me explain it this way," Scott said. "You want social studies teachers to teach persuasive reading of an editorial. But they won't. So tie the social studies teachers' evaluation to the students' language arts scores. You want phys. ed. teachers to teach caloric intake vs. calories burned by exercise. But they don't. Tie the P.E. teachers' evaluation to their students' math scores."

"What will Union Boss Kaifes have to say about that?" Jill asked.

"Nothing in the teachers' contract language mentions test scores. Let Kaifes fight it out with the Board of Ed. If the Board changes its mind because it's afraid of the teachers' union, then test scores are off the table, and we win either way."

Scott wasn't finished. "It gets better. The Board has agreed to use a growth model for individual student test scores. So little Johnny's test scores in 5th grade will be measured against little Johnny's test scores in 4th grade. Every child makes year-to-year progress, even if that child doesn't reach the benchmark. We all know that."

"Once the Board sees that in your building or department every child's test scores have risen for the year, we have passed that evaluation marker, and the Board has agreed to pay us a 5% raise for each year of that progress."

"That's going to cost the Board a lot of money," Bobby Jones, still smiling, said.

"Exactly," Scott concluded. "We get to construct the scoring evaluation categories, and then we get the big raise once we've met the evaluative criteria we've constructed.

The Board has no idea how much more expensive this idea of merit pay is going to be."

"Son of a gun," B.J. Cox cooed. "Scott, you do have this all figured out. Maybe we need to discuss this further at the Irish Rose pub after this meeting ends.

Perrillo blushed. The others in the room groaned.

"One more thing," Perrillo said. "On a very serious note, as you know our colleague and middle school principal, Doug Durling, has been diagnosed with lung cancer and has concluded his treatments. I spoke with his secretary at the middle school today. His most recent tests were bad."

"How bad?" Rosemary Grogan-Unangst asked.

"Hospice has been called," Perrillo said, looking at his shoes.

The room groaned again, this time in despair. Contract negotiations suddenly seemed small and irrelevant.

TWENTY

THE ASSISTANT SUPERINTENDENT

Although Lilly Laboy had retired as of January 1, she was still being paid by the Menlo Grove school district on a per diem basis for her work on "special assignments" for acting superintendent Michael DelVecchio.

The Board of Education agreed, voting 7-2 in favor of this arrangement. The only dissenting votes came from Larry Griffiths, always dressed in tweed and now embracing his growing reputation as a curmudgeon; and from Suzee Semanski, nurturing her reputation as a curvaceous contrarian to all things DelVecchio.

DelVecchio was especially happy with the arrangement because, even though Lilly was a two and a half hour ride south to the Shore, he would now have a good excuse to call her every day to ask her advice.

Two "special assignments" Lilly had been working on for the district included the Danny Wells alleged bank robbery, and the never-ending tenure case involving the incompetent elementary school special education teacher. Lilly also agreed to visit the central office once each month to catch up in person with DelVecchio.

Lilly walked into the central office building and headed directly to DelVecchio's office. He was waiting for her when she entered the room.

"What's new?" she asked.

DelVecchio sat silently for a moment, staring into space. He refocused and looked directly at Lilly. "Tony Martino will resign his Board seat at the next meeting."

"You're kidding! What's going on?" she asked.

DelVecchio answered as if reading an official statement, "He wants to spend more time with his family."

"Bullshit, Michael. What's going on?" Lilly had been around Menlo Grove too long to believe DelVecchio's statement.

"I might need his vote for my new contract," he said solemnly. "Tony can't be one of my five votes I must have for my new contract because his wife works for the district. He is going to resign and the Board will choose a replacement who can vote for me."

"How can you be sure the replacement will vote for you?" Lilly leaned forward in her seat.

"That can be arranged," DelVecchio softly said.

"Why are you so worried anyway? You have your five votes without Tony. Only Larry and Suzee will not vote for you."

"The Board election might not go well. Debbie, Tony, and Daniel are up for reelection. Tony can't vote, so we'll replace him. Daniel can't vote for me because his entire family works for the district. That means I need five of the remaining seven members who can vote. If Debbie and Tony's replacement both lose their reelections, I'm left with only three yes votes."

Lilly closed her eyes and thought hard.

She began whispering to herself. "Board president Bill Burton and vice president Vito Viterelli were automatic yes votes for DelVecchio. Carla Casella, science teacher, would probably vote yes. Margie Steinmetz, the most honest person on the Board, could go either way with her vote. That was three definite yes votes. Debbie Duhan and Tony Martino's replacement were the other two yes votes, but both had to win reelection first. If they lost, DelVecchio only had three certain votes, maybe four if Steinmetz voted yes."

DelVecchio was right.

Lilly eyes opened and suddenly realized something else. If DelVecchio could not gather the five votes to approve a new contract, he would be out of work and his long career in Menlo Grove over. Lilly Laboy's extended career, and more importantly to her, her influence in Menlo Grove, would also come to a sudden end.

She could permanently live at the Shore and would soon be forgotten in Menlo Grove. The thought made her shiver.

Lilly agreed to meet Union Boss Kristoff Kaifes at the yearly non-tenured teachers' dinner before heading home. She had driven north from the Shore very early in the morning and spent the day visiting her mother, still living in Menlo Grove.

Before heading back home to the Shore that night, she would talk to Kaifes about what to do with Danny. The youngest Wells, son of Board member Daniel Wells, had been unable to make it with the fire department, but hired as a favor by the Board of Education as a building and grounds worker. Danny Wells had been accused of robbing a local bank. The thought still made Lilly shake her head in astonishment.

The other building and grounds workers involved had been already fired, but Danny's case was being delayed, according to the blogs, because of his relationship with the Board. And his father was running for reelection.

Lilly entered the ballroom as Kaifes was concluding his remarks to the new teachers in the audience. All the teachers were in their first three years as employees in the district, meaning that without tenure, they could be fired for any reason.

Non-tenured teachers had been known to be non-renewed for failing to work after hours as coaches, club advisors, or as extra office help. These reasons were never mentioned, of course, in their final evaluations, but all teachers knew if you were not tenured you either did whatever the principal told you to do or risk being non-renewed.

Sometimes it seemed one's classroom effectiveness was only part of the evaluation. Making the principal happy was another part. The principals, of course, needed to keep the superintendent happy. And superintendents were subject to the whims and political winds facing the Board of Education members. This became especially true once the state removed tenure protection from superintendents.

Kaifes, relaxed, held the microphone in hand like he was an after hours lounge singer. He suddenly began warbling, "And I say this union will stand behind you new teachers all the way. We will protect your rights. We will not allow the Governor, the state legislature, or the Board of Education to infringe on your rights to collective bargaining. We will not allow anyone in the Statehouse to change your pension or change your tenure rights. "

"But you must vote. You must exercise your right to vote and you must vote for the right people. You must vote for the people who will protect your rights from those who do not care about you. From those who are trying to hurt you."

"You must be protected from those people who do not know how hard you work every day, every night preparing lessons for their children. From those who want to take money out of your pocket and give it to their big corporate donors."

"We will protect you, but you must become active in your association. And you must vote for the right people."

With those words serving as cue, a table of association reps stood up and walked to the many tables filled with new teachers. The union reps distributed full-color brochures with charts and graphs illustrating the voting patterns of each local, state, and federal representative for the Menlo Grove district.

At a table to the far left of the room, a young man with dark, tousled hair and wearing a collarless shirt, raised his hand.

Kalfes noticed the young man's hand. "Yes, a question."

The dark-haired young man spoke clearly. "How much truth is there to the rumor that there will be lay-offs this year because of the decrease in state aid to the district?"

"It is true the governor is underfunding Menlo Grove," Kaifes answered. "And I give all of you in this room my word that your association will do everything in its power to protect teachers from lay-offs."

The group of union reps stopped distributing materials and began cheering. Many of the new teachers followed their lead and also applauded.

Very few of them, full of energy, but overwhelmed with schoolwork and arriving home exhausted every day, had any idea that the governor had cut state aid to Menlo Grove by 60%. If the upcoming local school budget failed to pass the public vote, the defeated budget would have go before the town council. The town council had the power to cut even more from the budget if they desired.

Kaifes concluded his remarks, "But you must vote."

More applause followed from the crowd. Kaifes smiled as he returned to his table. He spotted Lilly standing against the back wall of the room. He walked past his table and toward her. Lilly's arms were folded. She was not smiling as he approached her.

"Hey, Lilly, good to see you," Kaifes said as he reached out his arms to hug her.

Lilly had known Kaifes since she had entered the district many years ago, so she stuck both arms straight out in front of her, locked her elbows, and held him back and off her. Kaifes, in turn, kept smiling as he held both his hands up innocently, like he was being held up by a thief, leaned over from his waist, and tried to give Lilly a short peck on her cheek, falling short by several inches.

"Hello, Kristoff," she said. "I stopped by on my way back home. We agreed to touch base on the Wells situation."

"How's retirement?" Kristoff asked.

"Hey, it's 8:00 P.M. and I'm here. So who's retired? What are we going to do with Danny Wells?" Lilly inquired bluntly.

"Do whatever you want with him," Kaifes responded.

Lilly blinked once. She stayed silent.

Kaifes filled the void. "His old man on the Board is making noise about cutting this and that from the budget. My God, DelVecchio already cut three million just to try to get the public to vote for the damned thing. The Governor going after us is one thing; but having Board members trying to take even more is too much. If old man Wells wants to play to the public just to get re-elected, fine. You tell DelVecchio he can fire little Danny and the association won't say a word."

Lilly looked shocked. "Are you sure?"

Kaifes looked her straight in the eye. "If Daniel Wells won't play ball with us, he can find his bank robbing son a job with somebody else."

"I'm a little surprised," Lilly admitted.

"The association can find other Board candidates to endorse, and those candidates will be happy to get it."

Now it was Kaifes who wasn't smiling.

Lilly's cell phone started vibrating in her purse.

"Hello? What is it, Charlie?" she asked her husband on the other end.

"I am leaving now. I should be home about 10:30," she said with exasperation.

After closing her cell phone, she said good night to Kristoff, left the building and walked to her car in the parking lot.

Three questions would not leave her mind as she started the car:

Did her husband call her because he was worried about her driving the freeway at night, or still trying to control her movements as he did when she worked full time?

Or did he just want to know how much more time he had to play before she arrived at the Shore later that night?

And what on earth was going on between the teachers' union and former teacher and current Board member Daniel Wells?

TWENTY-ONE

THE NEW GUY

Michael Ferrone thought Lilly Laboy's retirement would mean he would be free of her constant oversight and second-guessing. Her absence from central office, however, did not change her having DelVecchio's ear on every topic dealing with nearly every issue, including curriculum and instruction.

Ferrone's latest meeting with Acting Superintendent DelVecchio exemplified their relationship now that Lilly's physical presence had gone.

Ferrone walked into the over-sized, dark office of the Acting Superintendent a few minutes after 8:00 A.M. DelVecchio sat behind the large desk and looked down at the morning newspaper.

"Good morning, Mike," Ferrone said. "I have a memo to release to the elementary principals, but want to run it by you first."

Ferrone handed DelVecchio the one page memo containing five paragraphs.

DelVecchio didn't look at it. "What does it say?" DelVecchio asked.

"Not much," Ferrone answered. I've been working with Lucy on the elementary curriculum. As you know she and I have done training with the principals so we can get them all on the same page."

"I know that," DelVecchio responded, now squinting and frowning at the memo.

Ferrone continued, "The memo just states that now our training is completed, the Division of Curriculum and Instruction expects all principals to hold their teachers accountable for teaching the district curriculum."

"Why is this memo so long?" DelVecchio asked.

"I summarized each step of our training and what my expectation is for the principals," Ferrone explained.

"The principals answer to me, not to you, you know that," DelVecchio stated clearly.

"I know. That's why I want to clear the memo with you and make sure you and I are on the same page regarding the principals' fidelity to the elementary curriculum. Is it okay to send out?"

"Let me think about it," DelVecchio said. "Anything else?"

"No, that's all," Ferrone replied, a bit confused.

'Okay, thank you," DelVecchio concluded, setting the memo aside and returning his attention to the local daily newspaper.

As soon as Ferrone left the office, DelVecchio picked up his cell phone and hit speed dial #2: Lilly Laboy.

At 1:45 P.M. that afternoon as Ferrone worked in his office reviewing unsatisfactory teacher evaluations in preparation for non-renewals, he heard the side exit door open and someone enter. A second later DelVecchio stuck his head in the doorway of Ferrone's office.

"Don't send that memo," DelVecchio directed.

"Okay. What's wrong with it?" Ferrone asked hesitantly.

"The elementary principals know what they're doing. Each of their schools has its own needs," DelVecchio's face looked grim.

"I still think it's important we get them to make certain their teachers adhere to the district's curriculum. Lucy tells me some of those buildings are all over the place in instruction. Some of those principals completely ignore any direction from this office," Ferrone realized he had stepped over the line by continuing the line of persuasion after DelVecchio had issued his order.

DelVecchio, unperturbed, simply walked away saying, "That memo is way too long."

Ferrone took a deep breath, closed his eyes once to calm himself, knowing full well that the Superintendent was the boss; he called the shots. Then, just as quickly, he remembered and grimaced: he would have to tell Lucy that the memo would not go out to the elementary principals.

Ferrone wondered what Lilly had said to DelVecchio to convince him to make his decision.

This was getting old. He decided to call Lilly himself. He quickly dialed her number before he could stop himself.

"Hello?" Lilly said.

"Hi, Lilly, this is Ferrone. Sorry to bother you. You remember that Lucy and I did some training with the elementary principals to make certain everyone is on board with the district curriculum."

"Yes, I know," Lilly said, clearly taken aback by the call.

"I want your opinion as the former Assistant Superintendent of Curriculum and Instruction. What do you think of my sending out a memo telling them that they would be held accountable for their teachers teaching the curriculum this office has approved?"

Lilly stayed silent for a moment on the other end of the phone.

"Uh, well, I think you need to talk to the principals about that," she finally said.

"What do you mean?" Ferrone asked.

Lilly quickly organized her thoughts. "If someone were to ask me about a memo from you," she began, obviously seeing right through Ferrone's question, "I would tell that person to talk to some of the elementary principals."

"Oh," Ferrone muttered.

"And I would tell that person to talk to some of those principals first to protect the writer of that memo. You know, Michael, some of those elementary principals have their own agenda. You have to be careful. They can hurt you," Lilly advised.

"Oh, okay. Yeah, okay. Thanks, Lilly. Thanks for your advice. How is everything going with you?" he asked.

"Everything will be fine as soon as we can settle this tenure case," Lilly replied. "Then maybe I can really retire."

"Yeah, tell me about it," Ferrone responded, knowing he sounded patronizing. "Thanks, Lilly. Bye."

Ferrone hung up the phone. The call had educated him in several ways:

First, the elementary principals had succeeded in undermining Lucy's curriculum work once again; next, he knew Lilly Laboy loved the feeling of power she had with DelVecchio, and was in no hurry to give it up; and finally, DelVecchio would find out from Lilly that Ferrone had called her to ask about the memo.

"Damn it," he said under his breath.

He stood and stretched. He needed to walk to Lucy's office and tell her the memo had been squashed.

On his way, he stopped by the office of the Director of Student Services, now occupied by Abha Patel, newly promoted from middle school teacher, and about twenty-five years younger than Ferrone.

Patel's secretary was not at her desk when Ferrone arrived, so he stuck his head into Patel's doorway. Her head was barely visible amid several large stacks of white paper.

"Hi, Abha, how's it going?'

Patel looked up. Her wide eyes grew wider. Her lip quivered. "Fine. Fine," she said. Her voice trembled.

"You are going to be okay," Ferrone offered.

Patel immediately burst into tears.

"It's all right," he said.

"No, you don't understand. I just found out that two male coaches who are special ed teachers took one of the paraprofessional ladies out for drinks on Friday."

"There's nothing wrong with that," Ferrone said.

"But it was one of the older ladies. She's about fifty-five," Patel sobbed.

211

Ferrone shifted in his seat. He had just turned fifty-seven.

"She is divorced, always looking for a boyfriend, and apparently there just aren't that many available men in that age group."

"Okay," Ferrone seemed hesitant to continue this conversation.

"Well, those two idiot twenty-somethings got her drunk. They got her drunk and had sex with her. Both of them!"

Ferrone quickly closed the door behind him and sat down in one of the chairs. This was not a topic for the ears of eavesdropping secretaries. Now he was really uncomfortable. He quickly decided to change the subject.

"You have some mess to clean up in this division," Ferrone said, wondering if DelVecchio knew about the coaches and the para.

The young Assistant Superintendent began crying again.

"It's okay, Abha, you can do this. I feel the same way you do every single day."

She stopped crying and looked at him. "You do?"

"You have no idea," Ferrone offered. "I don't have the mess that you do, but I get the feeling I am being undermined every single day I am here."

"You do?" Patel asked again. "But you have worked in education for such a long time."

"Hey, take it easy," Ferrone joked, fully aware of his veteran status in the business, and sensitive about the "older lady of fifty-five" comment. "Don't rub it in."

"I don't know if I can do this job," she said softly.

"Of course you can. Every new job has a learning curve. You're fully qualified. You went back to school and got your certification. You have worked in special education for over a decade." Ferrone started again sounding like a coach giving a pep talk.

"Besides all that, you're smart. You'll learn this stuff in no time. Have you talked to Lilly about this mess she left you?"

Abha Patel smiling. "Every day. Lilly has been very good," she said.

"There you go. Lilly has been a big help to me as well," Ferrone said with a straight face.

"I cannot believe all the missing paperwork, and all the numbers that don't add up. Sometimes I think there are numbers here that have been fudged!" With this statement, she realized she may have said too much, and her dark eyes looked right and left, as if she feared someone would hear her words.

"You hang in there," Ferrone said to her, getting up to leave, also realizing the young Assistant Superintendent may have said more than she wanted. "It's going to be fine."

"Thank you, Mr. Ferrone," she said as he left her office.

"Please call me Mike," he said as he disappeared around the corner, exhaling loudly.

"She's in way over her head," he thought to himself as he continued to Lucy's office.

When he entered her office, elementary supervisor Lucy Williams looked up and quickly grabbed her blazer hanging on the back of her chair and put it on. Ferrone noticed, but pretended not to and said nothing.

"I need to talk to you about our training with the principals," Ferrone began.

"Oh, I know all about it," Lucy said. "My friend Christine - who was a trainer with me way back when – she called me after she talked to Rosemary Grogan-Unangst. I know the three she-wolves all got calls from DelVecchio about your memo."

"Gee, news really travels fast here," he said, a bit dumbfounded.

"Oh, you have no idea," Lucy commented while trying in vain to button the straining blazer.

"What do you think we should do?" Ferrone asked.

"You know what? Fuck it. Fuck them. Fuck the whole thing."

Ferrone eyes got wider. He had never heard Lucy swear before. What was going on around this place?

"Besides," she continued. "If the Board election doesn't go well, DelVecchio is out and who knows what will come next. I am getting too old for this."

Ferrone thought, "Again with the age." He knew Lucy and he were about the same in both age and years in the business.

Suddenly, Lucy stood up, took off the blazer, and placed it carefully on the back of her chair. When she sat back down, Ferrone noticed her cheeks had turned crimson.

Ferrone smiled. He removed his own suit jacket and threw it against the office wall. He looked at Lucy. "You're right, Lucy. Fuck it." She began laughing and looked at his suit jacket lying on the floor of her office.

"You're getting too old to do that," she giggled.

"You're absolutely right." He grinned back at her while he picked up his jacket and folded it over his arm. "You're busy. I just wanted to let you know about DelVecchio, Lilly, and the three she-wolves."

"Lilly? What does Lilly have to do with this?" Lucy asked.

"I called her to find out about why the memo got squelched. I found out DelVecchio called her about whether or not I could send the memo to the principals. She advised him to call the three she-wolves," he said bluntly.

"Oh my, God. I don't know how you're managing to deal with all this crap."

"Crap?" Ferrone said smiling. "Lucy, that's the first time I've ever heard you use such language. Do you think it's appropriate to say 'crap' in front of the assistant superintendent?"

He could still hear her laughing heartily as he walked down the long hallway and back to his office.

TWENTY-TWO

THE INTERVIEW COMMITTEE

A special meeting of the Board of Education had been called to replace Tony Martino, who had suddenly resigned without warning at the regularly scheduled meeting two weeks ago.

Martino, Deputy Chief of the Menlo Grove police, read a prepared statement regarding his decision to resign effective immediately to spend more time with his family. He thanked his fellow Board members, and expressed appreciation to Michael DelVecchio, Acting Superintendent.

Following the reading, Martino stood up and walked directly up the aisle and past the slack-jawed building administrators and citizens and out of the auditorium. He was almost halfway out of the room when the other Board members began clapping. A few audience members joined in amid their bewilderment.

Now, two weeks later, the remaining eight Board members would act as their own interview committee. Nine local residents, seven men and two women, submitted resumes and would be given three minutes each to explain to the Board members why they should be chosen to replace Tony Martino.

Each hopeful resident stood at the podium and all had prepared a statement of background and credentials. No questions were to be asked following each statement.

Board president Bill Burton was annoyed enough that he needed to attend this meeting; he had no intention of extending the agony by allowing a Q & A to occur.

Menlo Grove had a population of more than 100,000, and many who lived within the community possessed outstanding credentials. Of the nine who stood and spoke, there included three Ph.Ds, two business executives, one very successful entrepreneur, and three present or former school administrators. Overall, the group appeared more educated, capable, and articulate than the current Board members who would sit in judgment.

One Ph.D worked as a scientist for a large pharmaceutical in a nearby town. The second Ph.D lectured on urban studies at the state university, while the third was a best selling author who wrote on brain development. All wore dark suits, including the female lecturer.

Each articulated a vision for public education in Menlo Grove. Tweed-jacketed Larry Griffiths was practically jumping out of his seat yearning to ask a question, but BOE president Burton's no-question rule reigned, and Griffiths had to keep his questions and his excitement to himself.

The two business executives were nearly as impressive. Each had moved up the ranks of their organizations, understood management, and both held Ivy League degrees. Both wore dark charcoal suits and non-descript ties.

The entrepreneur, of Asian descent, had founded an internet service for business employees who worked remotely and with this service, could access charts and graphs in 3D. He wore an expertly fitted olive windowpane suit and maroon tie.

Two of the three educators were retired school superintendents. Each had served long and well, and wanted to share their expertise in the town where they had decided to raise their families a few decades ago. The man wore a blue pinstriped suit. The woman wore a smart, cream dress that fit a bit too snugly.

The third educator currently served as assistant principal of a high school in an adjoining community. He was big and beefy and bore a striking resemblance to Fred Flintstone. He wore neither animal skins nor a suit, however, choosing instead a pastel pullover and baggy blue jeans.

The Board listened patiently as each person read a prepared statement. When the final candidate concluded, president Burton announced to the small crowd in the audience that the Board would move to closed session to determine who would be selected to serve the remainder of Tony Martino's term. Since Martino's term expired in only a month, the new member would be active for only one meeting before the next Board election. After that, the new person would have to run for reelection to remain on the Board.

Forty-minutes later, the Board returned to public session and Burton read a statement to those who remained.

"The Menlo Grove Board of Education would like to thank and extend our appreciation for all of you who submitted an application for the vacated Board of Education position."

Burton continued, "The Board members are very impressed by the quality of the applicants. I would like to say, speaking for the rest of the Board, that we would like to see all of you attend our regular meetings. In addition to being pleasantly surprised by the credentials each of you possess, I must say I am also surprised that we have seen so few of you before tonight.

Please attend more meetings and continue to show your interest in getting involved in public education in Menlo Grove. If you aren't selected tonight, please consider running for a seat on the Board of Education in the future."

Burton paused and looked up at the audience as if he expected a reaction. There was none.

"Okay, let me congratulate and invite the Board's choice to complete the term to come forward toward the dais and take the oath: Mr. Roger D'Amico, currently assistant principal at South Rutherford High School. The silence that followed Burton's announcement was interrupted by polite applause, but most of those making up the audience looked at one another in wonder.

Mr. D'Amico stood up, and looking nonplussed, walked uncomfortably to the front of the room, where he took the oath from Business Administrator Dan Maris. The newest member of the Board of Education then took his seat at the far end of the dais. Since he had no members of his family employed by the Board of Ed, D'Amico could now do something Tony Martino would not have been able to do: D'Amico would be fully eligible to vote in favor of DelVecchio's new contract. First, however, he would have to win reelection, as state law mandated, much to DelVecchio's chagrin; a new superintendent's contract could be approved only after a Board election.

Almost immediately after having taken his seat, a night custodian appeared with a nameplate, and that nameplate had already been engraved with the name Roger

D'Amico. Some in the room found this quite interesting. No Board action in the past several years had proven so efficient.

DelVecchio and his allies on the Board had successfully replaced a non-voting member with one eligible to vote for DelVecchio's new contract. As long as Roger D'Amico could win election to the Board in his own right, DelVecchio had secured another yes vote. The fix appeared to be in.

TWENTY-THREE

THE ACTING SUPERINTENDENT

Michael DelVecchio, Acting Superintendent, sat at his desk and smiled. He had scored a political touchdown. He just replaced one Board member not permitted by law to vote on his new contract, and succeeded in having the Board appoint a new member who not only could, but also would vote for him. He had pulled off another political masterstroke. All perfectly legal.

DelVecchio had budget problems to resolve, but right now he wanted to enjoy this victory.

By replacing Board member Tony Martino with Roger D'Amico, DelVecchio now was closer to the necessary five votes needed to approve his new contract: Board president Bill Burton and vice president Vito Viterelli were sure yes votes. Science teacher Carla Casella and Margie

Steinmetz were two more allies of DelVecchio's, though Steinmetz could be a worry – the woman always insisted on looking on both sides of every issue – she was just too honest. That was four. DelVecchio needed a majority of the full Board. He needed one more.

The two no votes belonged to Larry Griffiths and Suzee Semanski.

Daniel Wells was a yes vote, but he had three family members working for the school district, so Wells was unable to cast a vote. Anyway, he was running for reelection and with the troubles he was experiencing with his son Danny, accused of a completely bungled bank robbery, and now with the union angry at him for his budget-slashing ideas, his reelection chances looked slim.

The other two members running for reelection were Debbie Duhan and, of course, the newly appointed Roger D'Amico. Both were solidly behind DelVecchio, but at least one of them would have to win reelection for DelVecchio to secure the fifth necessary vote. If either of the two: Duhan or D'Amico, won reelection, then DelVecchio would finally get his final big contract, and could at last drop the "acting" from his title.

Everyone would have to call him Superintendent DelVecchio.

This good feeling was offset, however, by the budget headache. Earlier, he and Board president Bill Burton had sat with business administrator Dan Maris and constructed a difficult budget. Because of the large decrease in state aid, much had to be cut from the budget before it went before the public for the annual vote.

The budget would be difficult to pass because the public seemed to be in a dour mood and against everything. Additionally, the union was upset because of the proposed cuts.

Even with the cuts, there was no guarantee the budget would pass. If it failed, the budget would then go to the town council for further review and possibly more cuts. Even though Mayor Kim had announced he would not be running for reelection, he would continue to serve until his term ended in the fall. His remaining in office until then and his remaining allies on the council could mean trouble for the budget, especially since his falling out with DelVecchio.

In addition, elementary school principal and town council president Rosemary Grogan-Unangst had resigned from the council two weeks after Kim's announcement that he was not running for reelection. That meant DelVecchio had even one fewer ally on the council. Because council members also had to run for reelection, there existed a great fear that if those running got their hands on a failed school budget, they would make a grandstand play and make an additional major cut.

Michael Ferrone, Assistant Superintendent of Curriculum and Instruction, stood at DelVecchio's door. DelVecchio had requested a meeting with Ferrone for two reasons: he wanted to inform Ferrone of the budget cuts in his division, and he needed to tell him that the principals were not happy with his leadership regarding the elementary curriculum.

Ferrone smiled as he walked in to DelVecchio's office. "Good morning, Michael. Interesting Board meeting last night. Some very impressive people applied for the Board vacancy. Curious the Board chose the person they did."

DelVecchio didn't know what Ferrone meant by curious, but he did know he did not like Ferrone's smirk.

"Sit down," DelVecchio said without emotion.

Ferrone sat at one of the comfortable chairs at the round table.

DelVecchio began reading items from a legal pad. "The budget going forward had to be rewritten due to the decreased state aid."

"Yes, I was waiting for someone to ask me what I thought could be cut."

DelVecchio glanced up momentarily. "That's my job," he said bluntly.

He started reading. "Full day kindergarten is out. We will have half day."

"That means the curriculum will have to be rewritten pretty quickly," Ferrone interjected.

"Then do it," DelVecchio answered brusquely. "That's your job."

We are cutting eighteen secretaries, one from each school and one from central office, six custodians, all middle school sports, intramurals, and clubs, ninth grade sports, and 150 paraprofessionals.

Ferrone stayed silent.

"From Curriculum and Instruction, your budget for textbooks is being cut from $1 million to $125,000."

Ferrone said nothing.

"Okay. What do you think?" DelVecchio asked.

Ferrone responded calmly. "Even after the first-ever district–wide textbook inventory we took last fall and the discovery of all those extra textbooks hoarded away in classroom closets, we cannot run our programs for $125,000. The math program for kindergarten to second grade costs us almost 100 grand all by itself. The books are all consumables and must be reordered every year." Ferrone knew cutting textbooks by nearly ninety percent was unrealistic.

"Why don't we just buy them a textbook?" DelVecchio asked.

"The publishing companies are too smart for that. The companies have all merged into just a handful. Nobody publishes a math textbook for kindergarten through grade two. They know if they did that, schools would just buy the books once and then copy the material."

"Well, you're going to have to figure it out," DelVecchio declared.

"Mike, the elementary schools alone cost far more than twice the amount you're allowing for the entire district. And we haven't even talked about middle school and high school."

Ferrone was looking straight at DelVecchio, but DelVecchio kept staring at his legal pad.

"You asked me what I think, so I'm telling you," Ferrone continued. "You cannot run your programs by cutting 90% from the textbook account."

"And, Mike, I don't say this just because it is a big number coming out of my part of the budget. I don't think it's a good idea because the public understands textbooks. When you cut textbooks, people understand what that means. I just don't think it's smart politically."

"It doesn't matter what you think," DelVecchio said. "And by the way, your entire budget for professional development is also being cut. We'll keep the in-service days, but no reimbursements for people who go out of the district for training, and no outside experts coming in. We'll use our own people."

Ferrone sat silently for a moment, "Okay, that's doable."

"Anything else you want to see me about?" Ferrone asked finally.

"Yes, one more thing," DelVecchio answered. "I'm getting complaints about you from the principals."

"What principals?" Ferrone asked.

"All of them," DelVecchio responded instantly without making eye contact.

Shocked, Ferrone did not respond immediately. He knew that was not true. His working relationships with both high school principals could not have been better. Instead of having the two principals meet with him at the central office, he met with them in their own buildings so at least one of them could be available instantly if needed.

The middle school principals and he met monthly as he sounded out their concerns. Many of the elementary principals regularly called him, confidentially of course, to share their thoughts and explain why they couldn't speak up more in front of the three she-wolves or DelVecchio. The only principals Ferrone knew who continually undermined him were the three she-wolves. Ferrone knew it, and he knew that DelVecchio knew it, too.

"It's not all the principals," Ferrone rebutted.

"All of them," DelVecchio repeated, emphasizing "all."

"You are trying to be too damn 'collaborative.'" DelVecchio said the word like it left a sour taste in his mouth.

"You knew I was collaborative when you hired me. This is the model I brought with me. It is what works."

DelVecchio didn't appear to be listening. "You need to be more directive."

Ferrone protested, "Mike, I have directed the supervisors to take an inventory of all texts - that was never done before - to do department training themselves, to check lesson plans, and they are taking on more and more of the observation and evaluation of the tenured teachers.

The principals are happy with what I have the supervisors doing."

This comment about the evaluation of tenured teachers surprised DelVecchio.

"Tenured teachers?" he asked. "The supervisors are also observing and evaluating the tenured teachers? Then what the hell are the principals doing?"

"Mike, they have buildings to run. And besides, "Ferrone added smiling, "the principals don't report to me."

DelVecchio did not return the smile.

"Okay, thank you," he said.

Ferrone left the office.

DelVecchio, clearly angry, thought to himself, mimicking Ferrone, "People understand textbooks. It's not politically wise."

"What does that piss-ant know about Menlo Grove politics?"

TWENTY-FOUR

THE MAYOR'S OFFICE

Today the people of Menlo Grove would vote either for or against the school budget, and for three Board of Education members. Three women, running as a team against the current administration and against the current Board majority, had challenged the three incumbents.

There would be no repeat of the previous year's election, when nine challengers to the Board's incumbents split the anti-Board votes and therefore, guaranteed majority control for the DelVecchio allies.

The three challengers this year had directly questioned DelVecchio's leadership and made constant references to the mysterious way DelVecchio had come to power, as well as what they considered the spendthrift ways of the current administration.

These three clearly supported Larry Griffiths and Suzee Semanski, the two current Board members who opposed DelVecchio's desire for a new contract. If the just two of three won, DelVecchio would be denied the five votes he needed to approve his new contract. With home foreclosures in Menlo Grove at an all time high, and many homes and apartment units sitting empty, the timing for the message of wasted taxpayer dollars could not have fit the public mood better. DelVecchio needed both Debbie Duhan and Roger D'Amico to win reelection. Despite the fact that the union endorsed both, DelVecchio's vulnerability suddenly looked real.

Mayor Kim may have decided not to run for reelection due to the intra-party challenge, but he felt perhaps the last laugh would be his before he left office in the fall. Town council member Rosie Ravioli automatically became the prohibitive favorite to become Menlo Grove's next mayor in this one-party town, but her promises to the teacher, fire, and police unions were not going to be sustainable in the current economy and the public's dour mood.

Kim was certain Ravioli's promises to the union bosses could not possibly be kept. He knew the public had soured on anything connected with public employees, and he knew the town council members, even those who did not support him, would want to make it look like they were playing hardball with the schools. Those council members could do so by threatening to cut even more money from the school budget if it was defeated. That was music to much of the public's ears.

Kim felt certain the school budget would fail, and he also knew the town council had a C.P.A. hired to review the school's finances. Any C.P.A could find questions within any budget, and could turn those questions into statements seemingly proving the school's mismanagement of the taxpayers' dollars. Many people in town, none of them knowing anything about running a modern and large school system, seemed predetermined to believe the schools were wasting money.

By constantly questioning the school district's use of tax money, the town council members were assisting in helping the budget fail. Once it did fail, the C.P.A. would write an official report stating the Menlo Grove School District had constructed a school budget, even with the cuts forced by the decrease in state aid, full of waste of unnecessary expenses.

If the school budget did fail, the C.P.A.'s document would give the town council members political cover to cut the school budget even more. Even if DelVecchio got his incumbents reelected, the budget would be so crippled, he and his team were doomed to fail and be subject to further public criticism.

Kim would await news of the election outcome at home. DelVecchio had treated him like he was an inter-loper in Menlo Grove politics, and had worked with Ravioli to undermine any changes Kim wanted to implement in the way business was done. But as short a tenure as Kim's reign as mayor may have been, the mayor knew the town council could leave DelVecchio with a gift of revenge that could end not only his even shorter tenure as Acting Superintendent, but his long career in public education.

And if the public schools in Menlo Grove had to take a hit for a few years, well, that was just collateral damage. The district was full of gifted kids and talented teachers. The schools would make a comeback. But Kim was certain that comeback would not take place with DelVecchio in charge.

TWENTY-FIVE

THE UNION BOSS

Kristoff Kaifes, President of the Menlo Grove Teachers' Association, scoped out the Board of Education meeting room. This room was commonly referred to as the "fish bowl" because it was surrounded on three sides by windows. Windows to the left faced the parking lot and outside world. Two other walls faced the interior of the building, so anyone walking along the adjacent hallways could peer into the meeting room and observe any proceeding occurring there. Just like every Board election each spring, the teachers' association leadership attended the vote tabulation held at the central office when the polls closed at 9:00 P.M.

Business Manager Dan Maris and his executive secretary received vote tabulations from the large town's thirty-two voting precincts. As the totals were received, Maris entered them into his computer, and the results could then be viewed on a large screen via a LCD projector.

Kristoff Kaifes and his band of deputies always attended this event. Normally, the number of attendees in Board of Education meeting room following a vote count would number about a dozen. Tonight, however, the room was completely full. Chairs had been set up in rows, making the room look like everyone had attended to hear a lecture. Every chair had a bottom filling it. Additional people, in whispered conversations, stood along the side and back walls, like late arrivals at an overcrowded Mass.

Most current Board members attended, even those not running for reelection. They sat in the front of the room. Those members running for reelection spoke nervously in voices above the rest. The three challengers stood together in the rear of the room, surrounded by local supporters and family. Nearly everyone checked his or her cell phone regularly.

Kaifes spoke with Board president Bill Burton, whose seat was safe, as he had been reelected the previous spring. However, every year following a Board election and subsequent swearing in of new members, a vote for a president and vice president occurred. If an election resulted in a number of new members, the possibility existed that new officers could be chosen as well.

"Hi, Bill, how are you tonight?" Kaifes asked Burton.

"Hey, I'm fine," Burton joked. "I'm not running tonight."

"What do you think will happen?" the Union Boss inquired.

"Why? Should I be worried? Burton asked rhetorically. "You told me your people put up signs all over town and made phone calls. If the teachers and parents come out, we'll be fine." Burton continued, "Debbie's nervous, though," as he nodded his head toward Debbie Duhan, pretty blond running for her fourth term on the Board.

Duhan sat in the third row next to Assistant Superintendent Michael Ferrone.

"I am so nervous tonight," she said to Ferrone in a voice just a little too loud.

Ferrone whispered in reply. "Not to worry, Deb. You won last time without the union support. This time they endorsed you."

"Yeah," she said, "I'm not so sure that's a good thing this time."

"Why do you say that?" Ferrone asked.

Duhan worked at a local florist shop and heard the talk around town from everyone with a birthday, anniversary, or death in the family. And the talk from Debbie's public gave voice to frustration and anger toward anything related to public employees.

"I don't know," she answered, "but suddenly, our teachers, cops, and firefighters are being thought of as the bad guys: underworked and overpaid. Never remember it this bad."

"Oh, teachers have always been thought of part time workers," Ferrone said. "I always figured it's because there are so many women who are teachers, many people think of teaching as 'women's work,' and that makes it easy and safe for a lot people to attack."

Debbie turned the topic to the subject at hand.

"But the public blames us as Board members for approving the contracts," she said. "They think teachers, who have college degrees, many of them Masters degrees, should work for peanuts. I'd like to see them try to teach kids."

"You're a good person," Ferrone assured her.

"I just hope I'm still a Board member after tonight. Those people running against us have no idea how complicated running a big district can be."

"Don't worry, Deb; don't worry."

Besides Debbie Duhan, another incumbent running for reelection was Daniel Wells, former teacher in the district whose wife and two sons still were employees of Menlo Grove, although the youngest Wells' son recently got himself involved in a legal entanglement involving the ill-advised and poorly conceived bank robbery. The third incumbent was the recently appointed Roger D'Amico, fulfilling the term after the surprising resignation of Deputy Police Chief Tony Martino.

At 9:20 P.M. the first results arrived via phone from the various and numerous locations of the voting precincts to DelVecchio's executive secretary sitting at her desk. She passed the numbers to Maris's secretary, who ran them into the Board meeting room, and gave the results to Maris. Maris punched the numbers into his computer, and the numbers then appeared on the big screen in front of the only solid wall in the room.

The initial set of numbers included three small precincts, all from the north side of town. The north side generally supported the school budget. The students from the north side did very well in school.

As the numbers showed the budget being rejected 2-1, Union Boss Kaifes muttered to Burton, "That's not a good sign,"

"It's only three small precincts," Board president Burton replied in a hushed tone. "But you're right; we usually win those three."

As the next three precinct results appeared moments later, an audible sound came from those in the room. Duhan clutched Ferrone's arm.

"Holy shit," she said. "Jesus, Mary, and Joseph!"

The results from the first three south side precincts showed the budget rejection rate at 6-1. Even worse, the three incumbents had fallen quickly behind the three challengers, though the numbers were still close.

Burton now turned to Kaifes. "A superintendent hates to get a budget rejected, but getting the Board you want is much more important."

"Well, neither of us wants those three housewives getting on the Board," Kaifes confirmed, alluding to the three women running as challengers. All three either had successful current professional careers or had retired from one.

Burton stayed silent as more results were being posted. He glanced at DelVecchio, who swiftly left the room and escaped to his office as the next three precinct results were shown on the big board. The office door closed behind him.

With half of the thirty-two districts reporting, the budget clearly looked in major trouble. More surprising, however, were the numbers themselves. Double the usual number of votes had been cast. In fact, with half the districts still to report, the total number of votes reported already equaled the total number cast the previous spring.

The three challengers had pulled further ahead of the three incumbents.

Duhan's anger and frustration rose in her voice. "I don't give a shit," she said. "I've done this long enough anyway," she said.

Ferrone said nothing. The numbers on the screen were doing all the talking.

All three incumbents were going down in flames. The Board was about to turn over. Board president Burton was the next person to leave the room, also via DelVecchio's office door. Union boss Kaifes paced nervously and uneasily across the back of the room, chomping on a mouthful of chewing gum.

"I'll tell you this," Debbie Duhan said to no one in particular. "I'm walking out of here with my head held high."

Ferrone reached over and held her hand, which felt cold as a February morning.

Kaifes suddenly found himself standing alone near the front of the room. He began a retreat away from the vicinity of business administrator Dan Maris, and approached the three challengers standing together with their families near the back of the room. The association had done more than not endorse any of the three.

The local union, to denigrate the three, had purchased radio spots, billboards, and innumerable posters and lawn signs. "Keep Menlo Grove Standards High", "Don't Turn Your Back on Our Children", "We Care About Your Children" highlighted each of the advertisements, as though the three challengers' goals would be in opposition to any of those empty statements. Below each slogan one could find the names of the three incumbents, all endorsed by the union.

Union supporters had written nasty comments on the local blogs about the three women challengers running for the Board. "The three housewives" became their common identity. Despite the effort and money of the union, right now the three challengers looked as if they were about to become new Board of Education members. Kaifes had to make a decision: make nice to the three apparent winners or declare all out war on the new Board of Education, which apparently would now include five anti-DelVecchio votes.

He blatantly ignored the three challengers as he walked directly past them, and he continued out the door of the building and into the parking lot. His posse of union deputies followed directly behind him.

War had been declared without a word being spoken.

TWENTY-SIX

THE PRINCIPALS

Board of Education elections generally only had an indirect effect on the people who ran the school buildings. If a budget failed, discretionary items in the budget would have to be reviewed and sometimes cut. Principals knew, however, that most items in a school budget were completely out of their hands: personnel costs made up 80% of a budget. Add transportation and the cost of running a building – fuel, electricity – and the amount of money spent of textbooks and supplies from a percentage of the entire budget measured just a small fraction.

However, if a Board of Education turned over – that is, if the number of new members elected in an annual election put the superintendent's job in jeopardy, then that proved a major cause for concern for the principals. Since Acting Superintendent DelVecchio only had two months remaining in his current contract, this concern heightened. A new superintendent brought all kinds of new questions and worries about the very direction of a district. The principals would have to begin again the process of proving himself or herself to a new boss who may very well have priorities completely different from the old boss.

Principals served an essential purpose in a school district: every day, all day, principals dealt with building management issues large and small. Children in their building were the ultimate responsibility of the principal. From the moment a child left the house to meet the bus in the early morning to the time that child returned safely to the front door, the principal was held responsible for the personal safety, social adjustment, and academic achievement of that child. School board members and budget votes occurred every year. Principals had more immediate and daily concerns.

Politically connected elementary principal Rosemary Grogan-Unangst called Cyndi Zubricki, fellow elementary principal and she-wolf, as soon as she entered her office the morning after the Board election.

The school budget had been defeated by 4-1 margin and the three Board incumbents all lost in their bids for reelection. Even though all three collected enough votes to win most Board elections, the voter turnout turned out to be so high for this election that the three had all been soundly defeated.

"Hello," Zubricki answered in her tired phone voice.

"Good morning, Cyndi," Grogan-Unangst said. "Didya' hear? The budget went down again."

Zubricki sounded distracted, and exhaled loudly, "Men!"

"What?" asked Rosemary.

"My husband is driving me nuts! I cannot take him much longer," Zubricki exclaimed. "He is a no good shit."

"Is he running around?" Grogan-Unangst asked. "Can't he keep it in his pants?"

"No, nothing like that," Zubricki responded.

"Did he hit you?"

"No, no, never."

"Oh, I get it. Verbal abuse. Does he get in your face and scream, calling you nasty names?"

"No, he doesn't do that."

"Drinking too much?"

"No."

"Refuses to keep up the outside of the house, and expects you to do everything on the inside, including all the cooking and cleaning?"

"No, he does his part."

"What then?" Grogan-Unangst found herself out of options.

"He walks too fast when we're together – walks way ahead of me, and he often drives aggressively."

"That son of a bitch! I think you should throw the bastard out."

Both women laughed, belying their concern about the previous night's voting outcome. Not only had the budget been defeated, but also Acting Superintendent DelVecchio's had lost his majority on the school board.

The two decided to call DelVecchio to find out when they could visit the central office for a face to face. They needed to know what last night's results would mean to their own professional futures at Menlo Grove. For the moment their concerns moved beyond the walls of the elementary schools they ran.

Meanwhile, that night, at Menlo Grove South High School, Principal Sam Applegate confronted his own issues. The letter regarding his high school building being labeled a "failing school" and the issue of school choice rose to the top of his priority list. Applegate busily greeted parents anxious to hear what this "School Choice" letter that they had recently received in the mail would mean to their children's academic futures.

Because an inordinate number of special education students had failed to pass the most recent state tests, the entire school was once again labeled a "Failing School" and therefore the students could choose to transfer to the high performing Henry Ford High School in the northern part of town.

The parents filled the old auditorium. Some stood along the side aisles, leaning on the walls. The crowd oozed an undercurrent of uneasiness and anger. Applegate and Assistant Superintendent Michael Ferrone, representing the absent Acting Superintendent, exchanged glances. Each wondered how this would end.

"Thank you all for coming tonight. I know you are anxious to hear about the letter you received in the mail about 'school choice'," Applegate began.

Applegate carefully outlined the options the parents had if they chose the inter-district transfer option, mandated by the state.

A parent in the third row raised her hand and stood up.

"But Mr. Applegate, I don't want to transfer my son to Henry Ford. And besides, he wouldn't let me even if I did want to. All his friends go to this high school. What I want to know is why are we put on this list just because some special education students didn't make the passing grade?"

"Those are the rules, Mrs. Smyth," Applegate replied calmly, smiling because he knew her from his attendance at her son's wrestling matches.

Someone near the back of the auditorium shouted, "That's not fair."

"No, it's not," Applegate said. "But we are not going to let the state label us a 'failing school.' Menlo Park South is a great school! We love our school! We are not Henry Ford High, and we don't want to be! We are Menlo Grove South!"

And with that, the crowd of parents dressed in jeans, T-shirts, and scuffed shoes, rose to its feet and cheered and whooped like sophomores at a pep rally.

As the meeting continued, Applegate explained, persuaded, cajoled, and schmoozed the audience. When the meeting ended an hour later, Applegate had saved Menlo Grove and Michael DelVecchio from a major headache. The number of student transfer requests turned out to be minimal. The scheduling, transportation, and room problems innate in a large number of transfer requests were avoided. Ferrone approached Applegate as the parents filed out of the auditorium and shook his hand.

"Great, great job, Sam. Man, I thought you were coaching again. Figured the next words out of your mouth were going to be, 'We're going to run inside; we're going to run outside,' just like Knute Rockne. Nice job."

Applegate smiled in satisfaction. "Dodged that bullet," he said, pulling out his cell phone. "I've got to call DelVecchio."

The phone rang and rang. DelVecchio never picked up.

TWENTY-SEVEN

THE BOARD OF EDUCATION

The three newly elected Board of Education members all appeared at the next meeting dressed in newly purchased dresses and shoes. Their families accompanied them, making the long walk down the center aisle of the auditorium and sitting in the front row. Husbands and children would assist by holding the Holy Book of choice during the official swearing in and photo-op.

Laura Benderman replaced the pert and vivacious Debbie Duhan. Benderman worked as an efficiency expert for a large technology firm. Recently, due to lay-offs, her job description expanded to include human resources and occupational safety oversight. Her greatest challenge as a new Board member would be finding enough hours to complete all her responsibilities at work, at home, and on the Board of Education.

Emily Wichniezak had defeated Daniel Wells, whose sons' behaviors helped undermine their father's re-election run. Wichniezak, like Wells, was a long retired teacher in the district whose late husband served as a district principal. Emily, however, had been on earth at least twenty years longer than Daniel Wells. Her greatest challenge would be staying awake during the late night Board meetings.

The third new Board member, Asshiyani Gupta, represented the new majority demographic in Menlo Grove. Her defeat of the one-month member Roger D'Amico, who replaced Deputy Police Chief Tony Martino after his sudden resignation, enabled her to become the first Menlo Grove Board member of Asian-Indian descent. Gupta was determined to break up the "good old boy" attitude that had been pervasive in town for as long as anyone could remember.

Following the swearing in of the three new members, the first decision of the new Board was to choose a new Board president and vice president. Current Board president Bill Burton asked for nominations. Board vice president Vito Viterelli raised his hand, was recognized by Burton, and making a very serious face, looked at the audience, and announced, "I nominate Bill Burton."

Suzee Semanski, current Board contrarian, raised her hand and before being recognized, said, "I nominate Larry Griffiths."

The older Griffiths, current Board crank and dressed as always in tweed, smiled demurely and raised his own hand.

"I would like to nominate Suzee Semanski as vice president," Griffiths said.

Burton frowned and scolded Griffiths. "We haven't closed the nominations for president yet, Mr. Griffiths."

Griffiths blushed. "Sorry."

"No problem," Burton said with quiet sarcasm. "Any other nominations for president?

No one spoke.

"Any other nominations for vice president?"

Silence again followed.

Burton broke the silence. "Well, I nominate current vice president Vito Viterelli."

Everyone stared straight ahead. The sparse crowd stared right back.

"All those in favor of Larry Griffiths for Board president?"

Larry, Suzee, and the three new members raised their hands.

"All in favor of me?"

Carla Casella, Margie Steinmetz, and Vito Viterelli raised their hands. Burton didn't bother to cast a vote.

"Congratulations, Mr. Griffiths," Burton wryly smiled.

Griffiths blushed again.

The vote for vice president followed a similar pattern. Griffiths, Semanski, and the three new members voted for Semanski. Margie Steinmetz broke ranks and voted for Semanski as well. The three others voted for Viterelli.

Griffiths and Semanski rose from their seats and advanced to Dan Maris, Board Secretary and the district's Business Administrator, who made the formal announcement and shook their hands. Griffiths moved to Burton's seat next to Acting Superintendent DelVecchio, who to this point had not looked up from staring at his hands. Semanski took Viterelli's place at the dais. Viterelli, in turn, took over hers without waiting to be asked. Burton, however, stayed at his place long enough to shake both Griffiths' and Semanski's hand, and then sat in Griffiths' old seat.

After a short public meeting memorable only for new Board president Griffiths' halting struggle through the agenda, the Board retired to closed session. Griffiths may have been elected new Board president, but during the closed session, DelVecchio and Board attorney Bob Butterfield facilitated a hasty rush through the agenda.

Griffiths sat quietly as DelVecchio announced, "We need to talk about our upcoming meeting with the town council to make our case so the council doesn't cut any more from our defeated budget."

"We've already cut it to the bone and the taxpayers still rejected it," Viterelli grumbled loudly.

"I think we should follow protocol," Griffiths suddenly announced. "No one recognized you to speak, Vito."

Viterelli's already limited patience had dissipated during the public meeting. The little man stood up, his face a shade of red similar to a Menlo Grove South cheerleader's skirt.

"You old bastard," he growled at Griffiths. "You don't talk to me like that."

And with that, Viterelli put his right knee on the table in a vain attempt to go over the conference table and grab Griffiths by his tweeds.

Griffiths' eyes widened and his face paled. The three new board members looked aghast. New board member and efficiency expert Benderman let out a small scream, Gupta shouted, "Oh, my God!" and the elderly Wichniezak raised her nodding chin and opened one eye.

"Take it easy, take it easy," DelVecchio roared. "This is still a goddamned Board meeting, and I am still the superintendent," he announced. "Let's act like adults."

Carla Casella assisted Viterelli, his face past red and now slightly purple, off the table.

Bill Burton, bemused, broke the tension by saying to DelVecchio, "That reminds me of the time you got so angry at Dan Wells, I thought you were going to break him in half."

DelVecchio now grinned in response. "Wells could get under my skin," he admitted about the recently defeated Board member.

Burton's smiled broadly, "You never liked him since the day he dropped that pass from you in high school."

DelVecchio stared in the distance at the memory, "Damned butterfingers!"

Everyone seemed to relax. The new ladies on the Board glanced at each other, and then looked at new Board president Larry Griffiths for direction.

Griffiths took the lead. "Okay, Suzee and I will meet with the town council about the defeated budget. Dan?" he looked at Maris, the business administrator, "will you join us? And Bill," Griffiths continued, looking at the former Board president, "I would like to have you there as well, since you and Mr. DelVecchio put this budget together."

"I would be glad to," Burton replied appreciatively at Griffiths' generous gesture.

Griffiths next looked at attorney Butterfield. "Bob, we have been going through this tenure case for over a year. What would it cost to cut our losses to make it go away?"

Butterfield pretended to peruse his notes. "We can get her to retire for a year's salary."

"This year's salary?" Griffiths asked.

"Well, officially, she would be on a paid disability."

Griffiths looked around the table at the others. "I propose we make this go away. Let's pay her off and finally get rid of her."

New member Benderman seemed about to raise an objection, but decided to hold her peace. No one in the room spoke.

"Okay, Bob," Griffiths directed the Board attorney. "Make this happen."

And with that, the Menlo Grove Board of Education successfully rid itself of an incompetent teacher at the cost of eighteen months of legal fees and an additional year of pay at the top of the guide teacher's salary guide for a non-existent disability to a teacher who would not and could not teach.

PART 4

FOURTH MARKING PERIOD

TWENTY-EIGHT

THE SUPERVISOR

The defeat of the school budget and the election of three new Board members, all opposed to offering Acting Superintendent DelVecchio a new contract, spelled uncertainty for elementary supervisor Lucy Williams. She welcomed P.E. and Health supervisor Bobby Jones into her office as she prepared herself a cup of tea.

"Good morning, Lucy," Bobby greeted her, knowing he needed to stay jovial to offset Lucy's sure to be surliness at the thought of the potential changes due to the recent election.

"Hi, Bobby," Lucy replied, sounding tired. "I'm just getting a cup of tea. The traffic was a monster this morning. Took me an hour and forty-five to get here, and I have to review a number of bad observations for a third year teacher in Rosemary's building. We may have to let young Miss Maureen Maddox go. If we keep her she'll get tenure, and then she's ours forever. Don't know why Rosemary even gave her a third year. Miss Maddox's first and second year observations were awful. It's obvious she cannot teach. May I make you a cup of tea?"

"No, no thanks, Lucy. No tea for me. Why did you and Rosemary recommend hiring this Maddox woman in the first place?

"I had nothing to do with hiring her. Rosemary told me the word came from the Superintendent's office to interview her and hire her. The first time I ever met her was during orientation." Lucy shrugged her shoulders. "It wasn't the first time that has happened, and probably won't be the last."

Bobby said, "I don't know how you've made that long commute all these years."

Bobby and Lucy had been teaching and supervisor colleagues for nearly thirty years. Bobby had been born and lived in Menlo Grove. Lucy never lived in the area, preferring a long and quiet long distance commute from the far reaches of the state.

"Well, I may not be making it much longer," Lucy offered.

"Are you thinking about getting out?" Jones asked.

"I think I'm getting too old for this, Bobby," Lucy replied. "If DelVecchio doesn't get a new contract, that means there will be a search for a new superintendent, and who knows how long that will take? Also, with the budget defeat and whatever additional cuts the town council made, I don't know how they expect us to run a school district."

She began weeping softly. "I can't believe they cut full-day kindergarten. That was such progress when we got it. This is a giant step backward."

Jones, uncomfortable with tears, tried to comfort her. "It sucks, I know, Lucy, but you'll figure it out."

"I don't know that I want to anymore," she said.

English supervisor Dina Thomas burst into the room. "Did you hear?" she asked.

"About what?"

"Sam Applegate's going to be fired."

"No shit?" Jones asked in wonder. "Applegate gone?"

Jones and Menlo Grove South principal Sam Applegate had coached together twenty years earlier when both were teachers at the high school in the southern part of town. Jones and Applegate, like so many who worked in the district, were sons of Menlo Grove with family connections to the political and educational reigns of power.

"Why?" Lucy asked, "The test scores?"

"That's the official reason," Dina Thomas answered. "But the word on the street is with the new Board in place, DelVecchio needs to get five votes for his new contract. The Board wants somebody to answer for Menlo Grove South being labeled a 'failing school.' DelVecchio is offering Applegate as the scapegoat to his new Board."

"Damn tests," Lucy whispered.

Dina continued, "DelVecchio figures if the new Board sees he is willing to offer up one of his own former football players and coaches for failing to get the test scores up, then he may still have a chance to get a new contract."

"No shit," Jones offered.

"Well, DelVecchio will never give up trying," Dina countered. "You know how stubborn he can be."

"Yes, that's for sure," Jones replied, stroking his chin and reflecting on his own days as a high school athlete under DelVecchio's regime as head coach.

"Replacing Sam Applegate as principal is not going to change Menlo Grove South's test scores," Lucy declared. "I can't believe anyone could be gullible enough to believe that."

"Believe it," Dina said. "But this gets better."

"What are you talking about?" Lucy asked.

"I hear that Abha is getting her pink slip."

"What?" Lucy shouted.

"No shit?" Jones asked repeated rhetorically.

"Come on, Dina, how can that be? She's only been on the job a few months. Why would DelVecchio want to get rid of her?"

"I hear Abha was a political choice. DelVecchio chose her as the new Assistant Superintendent for Student Services in an attempt to get the ethnic vote out in order to assure the Board incumbents would be reelected," Dina explained.

"Well, that didn't work," Jones added.

"No. If that was the thinking, then giving her the job did not help to keep DelVecchio's Board intact," Dina continued.

"So if Abha is not renewed, what will they do?" Lucy asked

"Apparently," Dina said, "a new member of the Board, Aashiyani Gupta, has a newly arrived relative with a friend who is looking to move into Menlo Grove, and this person has certification."

"But no experience, I suppose," Lucy offered sarcastically.

"So DelVecchio is firing one newly arrived ethnic to be replaced by another newly arrived ethnic, but this one has connections on the Board?" Jones simplified.

"Exactly," Dina agreed. "And not only that. DelVecchio told the Board he would do the Special Services job himself until the new person is hired and begins working.

"Oh, my God! They learn the game quickly around here," Lucy said. "Hiring someone with connections. Well, the more things change the more they stay the same. And DelVecchio is saying he can do the student services job AND be the superintendent?" Lucy rolled her eyes. "I've got to retire."

"You're retiring?" Dina screeched, thinking she had scored yet another scoop this morning.

"No, no, take it easy, Dina. Don't run out of here and start spreading more rumors."

"I don't spread rumors," Dina stated straightforwardly. "I only spread the truth."

And with that Dina Thomas, English supervisor, exited the room and practically sprinted toward the next open office door she could find.

Biff Pisano, supervisor of Art and Music, popped his head into the door.

"What's going on?" he asked.

"Same old shit," Jones replied.

"Would you like a cup of tea, Biff?" Lucy asked her fellow supervisor.

"Love one," Pisano answered, "though I think I may need something a lot stronger than tea."

"Why, what's wrong?" Lucy asked.

"I just came from DelVecchio's office. The place is like a morgue, and his mood is casting quite a pall," Pisano said.

"Exactly," Lucy confirmed.

"DelVecchio called me in to tell me that because of the additional cuts the town council made to the failed budget, my job is in serious jeopardy," Pisano's eyes suddenly were watery.

"But, Biff," Lucy said calmly, "how will that help?"

"DelVecchio is going to throw anything and anyone overboard to get his new contract. He is telling the Board what he thinks they want to hear. The new Board members got elected on the platform that the school district was top heavy at the central office, and with too much waste. So the old man thinks by getting rid of a supervisor or two and combining some jobs he can play up to those Board members and maybe convince them that he is the best person to be superintendent and get his new contract." Pisano looked exhausted.

"No shit?" Jones said. "But if they get rid of the Art and Music supervisor, who is going to do the observations and evaluations of the teachers in those departments; who is going to do all the orders and curriculum stuff you do?"

Pisano, the Art and Music supervisor, slowly looked up with tired eyes at Jones, the old gym teacher and coach. "You are," Pisano said. "P.E. and Health is being combined with Art and Music."

Jones' face turned white. He knew Pisano was telling the truth.

"No shit," Jones exhaled softly.

"No," Lucy corrected him. "It's full of shit."

TWENTY-NINE

THE ASSISTANT SUPERINTENDENT

Lilly Laboy, retired since January, had been receiving phone calls from Acting Superintendent Michael DelVecchio at least twice weekly in January, February and March. Following the budget defeat and the election of the three new Board of Education members in April, DelVecchio had called her incessantly for the first week.

Suddenly, since the new Board members were sworn in during the special Board meeting in late April, his calls to Lilly at her home at the Shore had diminished to one per week, and then once every two weeks. She found this healthy at first, figuring DelVecchio finally felt confident enough to make decisions without checking with her first. However, she had not heard from DelVecchio at all in the first three weeks in May. She decided to call him for an update on the latest in Menlo Grove.

DelVecchio's secretary picked up the phone, put Lilly on hold for a minute, then let her through.

"Hi, Lilly. How are you?" DelVecchio began.

"How are you, you mean?" Lilly countered. "I haven't heard from you. Is everything okay up there? How are you managing with the new Board?"

"I am managing just fine," DelVecchio said clearly. "New Board president Larry Griffiths is coming around. You know, it's easy to criticize when you're sitting all the way down at the end of the dais. But once you take your seat in the president's chair and have to run the Board meetings yourself, everything looks different. I am getting Larry to see things more clearly."

"That's good, Michael. How do things look for your new contract?"

"Things look good. I had to make some changes in personnel to make Board members happy, but I have my five votes," DelVecchio stated proudly.

"Changes? What kind of changes?" Lilly asked.

"I'm terminating Sam Applegate as principal of Menlo Park South High School"

"I suppose it all caught up to him. What was it, the drugs, the fights, the locked restrooms?" Lilly sounded only somewhat interested. She never found Sam Applegate much of an administrator.

"Well, all those things you mentioned didn't help Sam," DelVecchio explained.

"What was the final straw?" she asked.

"The test scores forced us to offer school choice. You remember that. We dodged the bullet on that one, as only a few kids actually wanted to change schools. But that got the Board's attention. They figured a new principal could improve the test scores."

"Michael," Lilly began, "you know better than that. You always said yourself you could switch all the teachers from Henry Ford High to Menlo Park South, and move all the teachers from Menlo South to Henry Ford, and the test scores would be exactly the same. I hope you didn't fire a principal just to appease the new Board."

"Listen, Lilly, the entire Board, old and new members, wanted something done. I am going to give them what they want. Applegate has worn out his welcome. I just have to write a final evaluation on him and end it."

"You haven't written Applegate's final evaluation yet?" Lilly asked knowingly.

"Well, actually, I was going to ask you to write it. You have written so many and you can really write. Would you write that evaluation for me, Lilly?"

"You know I will. You only have to ask. I still like to feel part of the team." This was about as close to schmoozing as Lilly could get. "Any other personnel changes I should know about?"

Oh, it turned out that Abha person you recommended for the student services position did not work out. She resigned two days ago."

"What? Wait a minute. Michael, that wasn't my or the committee's recommendation. You wanted her to meet some demographic concern. Don't you remember?"

"I took the recommendations from the committee. Anyway, she took the same position at West Brunswick. Do you believe that? She played us big time."

"What will you do now?" Lilly asked.

"Not to worry. I have another candidate ready to take over that position."

"How did you get a committee together so quickly? You didn't need me to do that? Did you have the new guy – Ferrone – handle it?"

"No, no. No need. I didn't need a committee. It would have taken too long. We had candidates ready."

"You mean the candidates from the previous interviews who didn't get the job?" Lilly was finding this conversation more curious by the second.

"No, none of the previous candidates fit what we were looking for. I chose someone from the outside."

"Oh, well, that's interesting. Where did you get the name? From the H.R. file?"

"No. Not necessary. Aashiyani Gupta, one of the new Board members, gave me a name. I interviewed the person and found her quite acceptable. The Board will vote on her at the June meeting."

Silence followed.

"Sounds like you have things in control without me," Lilly said softly.

"Don't be silly, Lilly," DelVecchio grumbled. "Things are moving quickly here. I didn't have time to call you every day."

"How did you make out with the town council after the budget defeat?" She asked. "Did they cut anything more?"

"Oh, didn't we talk since then?" DelVecchio seemed surprised. "Yes, that bastard Mayor Kim got his allies on the council to cut our balls off. They cut us another $6.5 million."

"What? You're kidding! Michael, how can you run that district with the lowered budget you set to the public, the $10 million less from the state, and now you're telling me the town cut the district another $6.5 million? That's almost $20 million less than this year!" Lilly Laboy had been in public education for over thirty years, but she had never heard of anything like this.

"Well...." DelVecchio began to get defensive now. He knew Lilly would not like what he was about to tell her.

"You know we went back to half-day kindergarten," he began.

"Yes, I know. That is a big mistake, Michael."

We also got rid of elementary World Language, over a hundred paraprofessionals, and because of the additional cuts from the town, we have to lay off all the elementary school non-tenured teachers."

"Get the hell out!" Lilly blurted out. "No new blood in any of the elementary buildings? You have so many old school teachers in the elementary schools now that are so difficult to change. What did Lucy Williams say when you told her that?"

"I didn't tell her. Lucy is the new guy's problem. He told her."

Lilly said, "I can't imagine she was happy."

"Hey, we had no choice. The class sizes will be way up even with the extra rooms we picked up with the elimination of full-day kindergarten. The teachers aren't happy either and neither are the parents. And I don't even want to tell you about the principals. But, you know, they should have gotten their parents to come out and support the budget. Oh, and we are outsourcing the subs and custodians." DelVecchio began to gain confidence as he repeated his oft spoken talking points to the bewildered Lilly on the other end of the phone.

"The new Board supports all this?" she finally asked.

"Hey, the public elected these people, and the public is going to get the kind of education they voted for in the election."

"But, Michael, you've spent over forty years in Menlo Grove as an educator. How do you feel about what's happening?"

"What do you mean?" he asked, completely unaware.

"The schools in Menlo Grove are going to go downhill. How are you going to feel about that?" She was almost pleading with him to see what he wouldn't see.

"I don't know what you're talking about," DelVecchio said into the receiver. "I work for the Board. I do what they say. They represent the people who voted for them."

"And you think that by doing the bidding of these know-nothings, you'll get your new contract." Lilly's tone clearly showed her disgust with this conversation.

"My concern is for the children of Menlo Grove. The district will bounce back. We have great teachers," he countered.

"Just not as many of them," she added.

"Lilly, I have to go. I've got a meeting with the Taxpayers' Association."

"The what?" she sputtered.

"The taxpaying voters. I am going to show them how I can give them an efficiently run school district," he said calmly.

"These people know nothing about educating children," she said slowly.

"Bye, Lilly. Got to go. I'll have my secretary send you some information on Applegate so you can write up his final evaluation. Thanks, Lilly."

Lilly heard the click while she held the phone in her hand. Michael DelVecchio had convinced himself that the new Board of Education would deliver the five votes necessary for his new contract and continued employment in the Menlo Grove school district.

And she was now convinced that he would do anything to assure that it happened.

THIRTY

THE NEW GUY

As Assistant Superintendent, some of Michael Ferrone's many responsibilities included overseeing the budget for all things related to curriculum: books, supplies, teacher training, and the supervision of instruction to assure teachers taught the Board-approved curriculum.

That meant when a budget needed to be cut, Ferrone needed to determine what items had to be reduced or eliminated entirely, and how the remaining funds were reallocated. Once DelVecchio had informed Ferrone that the money for textbooks was to be slashed to a tenth of the current amount, the first action Ferrone took was to call each supervisor into his office for a face-to-face talk about the new reality.

Since the new Board was elected six weeks ago, numerous people entered the side door of the central office building during the day, past Ferrone's office and into DelVecchio's. These people included the next mayor, Rosie Ravioli; former Board president Bill Burton; and former Board vice president Vito Viterelli.

New Board president Larry Griffiths preferred to meet DelVecchio for lunch in one of the town's many restaurants. The retired Griffiths let DelVecchio buy. New Board vice president Suzee Semanski refused to meet with DelVecchio. He was not counting on Suzee as one of the five votes needed for his new contract, but DelVecchio didn't care. He had the four old Board members' votes, and only needed one more, and he thought Larry enjoyed his new power as Board president and having DelVecchio confide in him. DelVecchio had already done much of what the new Board members wanted: fired a high school principal, replaced a recently hired Assistant Superintendent for Student Services with someone a new Board member recommended, and made cuts to programs like full-day kindergarten that even DelVecchio believed was worthwhile. He thought with these moves maybe even a couple of the new Board members would give him their vote as well.

Each supervisor arrived to Ferrone's office on time and equipped with a smile and a folder of order requests. As a former supervisor himself, Ferrone had a soft spot for them, and they knew it because he kept telling them. After years and years of getting nearly everything they had requested, the supervisors always knew if they arrived with a big enough "wish list" they could negotiate givebacks on items they knew they wouldn't get anyway.

When Lilly served as head of Curriculum and Instruction, she was so busy carrying such a big load, especially after DelVecchio's ascension, she would be only half-listening to the supervisors anyway. If she didn't have enough money in the budget, she would tell them that maybe she could secure some "Christmas tree" money – money politicos threw the school district's way as part of government pork.

This time everything was different. Ferrone's meeting with English supervisor Dina Thomas was typical of his individual meeting with each supervisor. Ferrone gave her the new budget number and told her of the elimination of money for out-of-district trainings. Thomas looked blankly at Ferrone and said, "I can't run my programs with that amount. And no money for training? You're kidding, right?"

"No," Ferrone answered. "That's the number we're working with. And that number is for the entire district, not just for English."

"What? I thought you meant that was my number. Michael, we can't run this district with such a small amount of money for textbooks. Did you tell DelVecchio that?"

"Yes, DelVecchio knows. I gave him the bottom line you and I agreed on earlier when we met last month, but he simply told me there was no money. We have to make do."

Dina Thomas's eyes widened. "Well, what will I tell my teachers? They expect to have the materials necessary to teach their courses."

Ferrone was ready with the central office line. "You tell the teachers that the district is spending so much on their salaries, benefits, and things like 'supplemental instruction' that there is no money left for their materials. Tell them to get creative."

"Oh, no, I'm not blaming their salaries and benefits. I don't want the building rep coming after me. And I certainly do not want to have a meeting with that union sleaze Kaifes. What do I say to the parents when they begin complaining that their little darling child has a dilapidated and out-of-date textbook?"

"Tell them they should have voted in favor of the budget."

"No one likes property taxes to go up," she responded.

"A failed budget does not bring taxes down," Ferrone replied. "Haven't they figured that out yet?"

"You need to talk to DelVecchio again. Do you want me to meet with him?"

"Listen, Dina. This is the reality. We have a new majority on the Board, and they think Menlo Grove has wasted millions of dollars every year. Talking to DelVecchio is not going to change your budget number. Besides, since the Board election, I haven't even seen much of him."

"What do you mean? You're right here." Dina leaned forward. The new guy was getting close to offering her some gossip.

"He is just very busy meeting with the new Board members and all. Remember, there is a new Board president. DelVecchio's job is to make the Board members happy. My job is to make the Superintendent happy. Your job is to make me happy." Ferrone was smiling now.

"And Dina Thomas, you are the best supervisor we have, and the best one I've ever worked with. Of course, I am biased."

"You mean because we were both English teachers? She asked.

Ferrone continued his kidding. "No, because I'm biased in favor of smart and attractive women."

"Oh, stop it," Dina, who just experienced birthday number 60, cooed.

"Do you want me to stop?"

"Of course not," she replied.

Ferrone got serious. "Work with me, Dina. Do what you can. I will keep looking for money. But remember, there is no more Christmas tree money. The governor's people are keeping a much closer watch on that stuff."

"You mean they are giving money to places who vote differently than Menlo Grove."

"Whatever, Dina. We can do this. You're the best."

And with that, Ferrone stood up, stuck out his hand, shook her hand and offered up one more appreciative smile. "You're my favorite, Dina." And then, whispering and grinning, he added what he told every supervisor, "Don't tell the others."

He thought to himself, "My God, I've been here less than a year, I cannot even stand myself."

This entire conversation played out similarly with every other supervisor, complete with the compliments about being "the best" and "my favorite." And every supervisor smiled, thanked him, and left the room.

The exception was Lucy Williams, elementary supervisor. When Ferrone told her he was biased toward smart and attractive women, Lucy, smart and attractive, looked directly at him and said, "Oh, really!"

Then she got up and left the room chuckling to herself.

Ferrone wondered, "What does she know that I don't?"

THIRTY-ONE

THE INTERVIEW COMMITTEE

As spring ripened, at Michael Ferrone's monthly principals' meeting at the central office, Acting Superintendent DelVecchio made his usual appearance. This proved to be the first time many of the principals had seen DelVecchio since the budget had been defeated and the three new Board of Education members had been elected.

At first glance it appeared DelVecchio had gone into hiding. However, Ferrone knew that although DelVecchio was spending an inordinate amount of time in his office, he was constantly either on the phone, meeting with the Board members who supported him, or buying lunch for new Board president Larry Griffiths.

When DelVecchio made his unannounced appearance by walking into the room, Ferrone stopped talking to the principals and attempted to make eye contact with DelVecchio to see if he wanted to address the group. Without bothering to look in Ferrone's direction, DelVecchio, in white shirtsleeves, began speaking to the principals.

"You know that I put together a reasonable budget containing $3.5 million in cuts for the Board to present to the public, and the public defeated that budget. Unfortunately, the state law mandates the defeated budget has to go before the town council for further review and possible additional cuts."

Everyone in the room already was well aware of all of this.

"The town council, at the behest of the mayor, who still has allies on the council…" DelVecchio glanced in the direction of Rosemary Grogan-Unangst. She had resigned from the town council when Mayor Kim announced he would not seek reelection, thereby denying DelVecchio a voice to fight the majority of the council in limiting further cuts.

Grogan-Unangst's cheeks reddened, but she stared straight ahead, refusing to blink.

"The town council, in their infinite wisdom, decided to cut us an additional $6.5 million. This has led me to make further program cuts."

Everyone in the room already knew this as well.

"I am going to be meeting with your association president to request all the principals and supervisors take a salary freeze for one year."

This was news to the association president and middle school principal Lou Ferrigno, who was sitting in the room.

"I am also taking a salary freeze, and have also told the assistant superintendents they would be taking a freeze as well."

The salary freeze was news to Ferrone, who was hearing about this directive for the first time.

"I am going to be looking for a limited number of new hires due to the budget situation. Only some of those retiring will be replaced. All recommendations for hire will take place here at the central office."

DelVecchio turned to Ferrone. "I need you to put together an interview committee for these few hires." He paused a moment. "I'll tell you who's going to be on this committee."

As the principals lowered and shook their heads, Ferrone smiled and looked at DelVecchio, who failed both to return Ferrone's look or see the irony in what he had just said.

"I know with the talented administrators in this room, Menlo Grove will continue to be the outstanding district it has always been, and I know I will be the one who continues to lead this district."

With that, DelVecchio's eyes suddenly moistened, and his voice broke. Everyone in the room was now staring intently at the older man standing in front of them.

He continued with tears in his eyes. "Together, you and I will continue to lead Menlo Grove." And then he turned quickly away and disappeared into his office.

The principals sat silent and shocked for a moment. Then the three she-wolves stood and began clapping loudly. The other principals were drawn into doing the same.

Ferrone sat staring in disbelief, looking stupid. He wondered if anyone else had ever gotten a standing ovation after announcing that everyone now applauding was taking a salary freeze.

When the meeting had ended, Ferrone dropped off his meeting materials in his office, and then stopped by to see if DelVecchio was available. He wanted to know who he was going to be told to choose for the interview committee he had been directed to organize.

DelVecchio sat in his office chair holding his head in his hands. When he heard Ferrone shuffling his feet at the office door, DelVecchio waved him in.

"Come in," DelVecchio directed.

"Who do you want on the interview committee?' Ferrone asked.

"Dan and I will handle the interviews," DelVecchio stated.

"What about the committee?" Ferrone looked and sounded confused.

"That is the committee. Dan and I will do the interviews. Thank you. That's all."

"Wait a minute, Mike. Dan Maris is the Business Administrator. You are the Acting Superintendent. Dan doesn't have any background in hiring teachers, supervisors, or whatever. And you don't have the time."

DelVecchio, still looking down, stood up. "That's all. Thank you."

When Ferrone returned to his office, he closed the door and sat down. He held his own head in his hands.

THIRTY-TWO

THE ACTING SUPERINTENDENT

Every Tuesday morning at 9:30, Acting Superintendent Michael DelVecchio held court with his "cabinet" of the central office administrators. He sat at the head of the long conference table with Business Administrator Dan Maris to his right.

Around the table sat the others, each sipping newly made coffee compliments of DelVecchio's secretary, and about half nibbling fresh pastry purchased and picked up by DelVecchio on his just completed morning drive and cigarette break.

Assistant Superintendent of Curriculum and Instruction Michael Ferrone sat opposite Maris, however the seat next to Ferrone remained empty due to the sudden departure of Assistant Superintendent of Student Services Abha Patel.

Her replacement would begin working on July 1. Next to the empty seat, Mike Fiorello, supervisor of attendance and security, chewed on a cinnamon cruller. Next to Fiorello, Peter Jenson, coordinator for building and grounds, joked with Sam Mussina, supervisor of technology.

On the other side of the table, sitting next to Maris, Brenda Dredahl, coordinator of testing, scribbled indecipherable notes. Next to Dredahl, Mike Smith, transportation director, whispered into his cell phone. A late-arriving child had been left at a bus stop in the southern part of town.

These seven, highlighted by four middle-aged white guys named Michael, may have represented the most popular boy's name in the post-war period, but they did not represent the demographic of present day Menlo Grove. Dredahl was the only female present, and she usually held her tongue when the men approached the edge of locker room talk.

"Okay," DelVecchio began in his usual low morning voice rumbling from his chest, "let's get started." Looking at the far end of the table he asked, "Mike, what'dya got?"

Transportation director Mike Smith quickly closed his cell phone and began to explain the early morning exploits of the district's 137 bus routes, 40 district owned busses, 22 rented busses, and 18 special education/handicapped vans. Even though hundreds of children were driven to school by their parents, a few hundred more walked, and most twelfth graders drove themselves, the district still transported nearly 10,000 students to and from school on a daily basis.

By law, school districts were responsible for providing transportation to anyone living more than two miles from a school. They also legally had to provide transportation for private school children living within the city limits. In fact, very few children in Menlo Grove lived two or more miles from a school building, but bussing had been provided to anyone wanting a ride for generations now. This was called "courtesy bussing," and whenever a budget failed, the first public threat made by a school district always involved the loss of "courtesy bussing." If someone lived 1.9 miles from school, the loss of courtesy bussing meant that person would have to find his or her child a way to school.

With the exponential growth in vehicular traffic and the breathtaking crisscross of interstate, state, county, and local roads located within the district, the thought of any child walking to school and attempting to cross a street during the daily madness made even the harshest critic of school spending shudder.

"We left a kindergartener at his bus stop this morning, down by Dell Road," Smith explained. No further description of the location was necessary because DelVecchio knew every street, avenue, road, terrace, and cul-de-sac in town.

"What are you doing about it?" DelVecchio asked.

"I sent the bus driver back to get the kid," Smith replied.

"Was the kid at the bus stop at the right time?'

"Probably not," Smith said, "but the mother swears he was, and said the bus driver deliberately left the child there. Of course, the driver denies ever seeing the child."

"Is the child in school now?"

"Yes, we got him to school. But the mom is probably lying and the bus driver might be stretching her story as well. You know, Mike, getting qualified people to pass the driver's and drug tests and get to work on time every morning is getting harder and harder because the pay stinks and there are no benefits. We have 82 drivers and 26 substitute drivers, and I swear, some of these people can't read "Stop" on their first try."

"Save it for another time. Not now," DelVecchio declared. "Anything else?"

"A few things. But I'll stop by later to tell you."

DelVecchio moved to the next person at the end of the table. "Sam," DelVecchio addressed the supervisor of technology, "what'dya got?"

Sam Mussina hated talking in public, even at a table with six of his colleagues. The perspiration began forming on his forehead as he began speaking.

"We just got twelve new computers in, and they are in the district warehouse waiting to be marked and delivered."

"Christ, Sam, you told me last week those computers had arrived. What the fuck, ah, er, excuse me, Brenda. What the hell is going on in that warehouse?"

Sam Mussina now started to stammer. "Uh, well, you see, Mr. DelVecchio, the guys down at the warehouse are constantly being called to different buildings to troubleshoot all the problems we've having with our old computers, and they don't have time to do much else."

"Shit, Sam, the Board wants to see some new computers in the school buildings," DelVecchio growled, knowing this made Mussina cringe.

"We only received twelve new computers, Mr. DelVecchio. We have seventeen school buildings. It won't make much difference," Mussina haltingly tried to explain.

"I want those computers marked and delivered today."

"Yes, sir," Mussina complied.

"By the way, which buildings are they going to?" DelVecchio asked.

"Three each to the two high schools and six here to central office," Mussina explained.

"Good, I keep having trouble with my email," DelVecchio said. "And send the old ones you take out of here to the elementary schools, like you always do."

"Yes, sir," Mussina said as he scribbled notes to himself.

This process continued as DelVecchio asked each member of his team what information he should know in case of a phone call from a Board member. Nothing, not lost children, not broken computers, nothing upset the Superintendent more than getting a call from a Board member and being blindsided by the forthcoming question.

It was up to each administrator present to determine what piece of information DelVecchio needed to know just in case.

Building and grounds head Peter Jensen complained he needed more money to try to fix the crumbling buildings worn by years of rowdy children and deferred maintenance. The school buildings in Menlo Grove were not just aging, they were aging gracelessly. Forty-year old buildings looked seventy; sixty-year old buildings looked ninety. Capital projects were delayed, cancelled, rejected in public referendums. Jensen would shrug his shoulders and rub his head.

Attendance and security director Mike Fiorello reported on the increasing number of homeless children the district was educating, and few more he had followed as they exited their bus and into to the waiting car of their mom, aunt, or mom's boyfriend. One such subsequent ride following a car took Fiorello out of Menlo Grove and into an urban area a few miles away. In a similar case one parent had given Fiorello's secretary an address that Fiorello found to be an empty lot where only a few abandoned car tires and a doorless refrigerator resided.

Next, test coordinator Brenda Dredahl read off aggregated test scores that made everyone's eyes glaze over until DelVecchio shouted, "Enough," causing Dredahl to look up in surprise and shut up in obedience.

"I'll stop by your office later," she murmured.

Without an assistant superintendent of special services currently on staff, the recent meetings lacked reports on out-of-districts placements which were costing the district millions each year, explanations of students mistakenly diagnosed, apologies for Child Study Teams unable to document services, and on and on. No special services report cut the weekly meetings by twenty minutes.

Ferrone offered a shortened version of his conversations with Board members serving on his curriculum committee, so DelVecchio would possess the exact same information Ferrone had shared with those Board members. Occasionally he tried inserting a comment about a new curriculum, training, or assessment initiative he had begun, but DelVecchio made no secret that these bored him, so Ferrone stopped trying to report those.

Board administrator Dan Maris was always the last administrator to speak, and he informed DelVecchio and everyone in the room that as a long time business administrator he had never experienced a budget situation worse than the current one.

Of course, DelVecchio and Maris spoke throughout the day as their offices sat adjacent and an open door welcomed conversation without either having to get out of his seat. Everything Maris said DelVecchio already knew as the two had already talked about what Maris would say in front of the others.

When Maris finished, DelVecchio glanced around the room, and then looked down at his folded and slightly yellowed shaking hands resting on the table.

"I have a few announcements of my own," he began. "As you know, next Monday night is the final Board meeting of the school year."

Everyone held his breath, as all knew DelVecchio's contract ended two weeks later on June 30.

"The Board and I have come to an agreement for my next contract." An audible exhale quickly rushed around the room.

"That's great, Mike," Mike Fiorello said.

"Congratulations, Mr. DelVecchio," Sal Mussina added.

Ferrone looked wide-eyed around the room. He glanced Dredahl's way, but she quickly dropped her eyes toward her notes.

DelVecchio continued, "We only have to agree on terms of my salary. Of course, since this will be the first of a three-year contract, and I only want three years, mind you, not five, I will not be taking a freeze."

The room stayed quiet.

"This is not for public consumption, so keep it to yourselves, but I wanted my team to know what was going on, since there has been so much speculation about my future. Well, I'm not going anywhere."

As he said the last sentence, Acting Superintendent Michael DelVecchio pounded the table one time with his right fist, stood up, and quickly exited the room. Dan Maris followed him out the door.

Everyone in the room had attended every Board meeting and the recent Board election, and everyone in the room knew only four remaining members of the Board could be considered supporters of DelVecchio. Everyone in the room also knew it took five votes for a superintendent to secure a contract, and everyone present knew the difference between four and five.

Where DelVecchio had found the fifth vote to ratify his new contract remained a mystery.

THIRTY-THREE

THE MAYOR'S OFFICE

A week earlier, Mayor Kim received word that the federal government would be sending no new money to the state for education. This served as a reminder that times had indeed changed and highlighted the announcement coming just a day later from state capitol. The Governor had decided to slash funding to local school districts because teachers "wouldn't take a salary freeze," according to the quote in the state's largest newspaper.

Kim wondered if the governor thought attacking the women who taught children how to read and understand math fundamentals would continue to be an effective political strategy. Rosie Ravioli sat visiting in the mayor's office, her legs struggling to cross as her feet barely touched the floor. Her hands were folded on her lap, and her mouth stayed tightly closed. Kim delivered the recent news from the capitol.

"The Governor's office has informed us that Menlo Grove's state funding has been cut by 60% from this year."

Ravioli finally spoke, making the obvious point. "The Governor must be aware that teachers' contracts were signed two or three years ago, and the district legally must pay according what the signed contract states."

"Of course the Governor realizes that, Rosie," Kim replied. "The governor is playing politics. The town must give the money to the school district so that all the contracts, not just the teachers' salaries, are funded. If we failed to do so, we would be sued and that would cost the taxpayers in town even more."

"Can you imagine," the mayor continued, "signing a contract with your plumber to renovate your bathroom, and then when he is halfway finished, telling him that you have decided not pay him what you had agreed to because you didn't have the money you thought you had? I don't think the plumber would take a "salary freeze," because that is not the way the legal world works. The Governor is a lawyer in real life, I seem to remember."

Ravioli understood completely. "The town has rejected the school budget. The town council will be reviewing the rejected budget to determine if more should be cut. Because of what the governor has done, I know you are going to say that the council leaves the budget as is. But I must tell you, Mr. Mayor, the council is going to have to cut something. To leave that budget without further cuts after it was voted down so overwhelmingly would jeopardize the council members' political futures."

"Political futures? Please, Rosie, spare me." The Mayor had little patience left for others' political futures, seeing how the majority of the council had ended his own. I not only agree with you, I am going to encourage the council to cut more. A lot more."

"You are still angry at DelVecchio," Ravioli said. "You are going to encourage the council to cut more to make sure DelVecchio doesn't get his new contract?"

"Listen, Rosie," the mayor answered, "Forget DelVecchio, he lost all three incumbents on his Board of Ed. He doesn't have the five votes needed for his new contract."

"I've heard he has persuaded enough Board members with his recent agreements with them so he does have the five votes."

The Mayor continued, "Believe what you want. Cutting the school budget even more is what the public wants. You said so yourself."

"What are you suggesting we do?" Ravioli asked.

"I say send a message to the public that you're listening. Cut that school budget to make everyone sit up and take notice of the town council."

"Well, that doesn't sound like you," Ravioli still seemed suspicious.

"Forget about me," the Mayor said. "My political career is over, thank you."

Ravioli looked down at her lap and smiled.

"But you cut that school budget and you will make a mark indeed." Now the Mayor also smiled.

"The town council is meeting with Mr. DelVecchio, some Board members and Business Administrator Dan Maris tonight," Ravioli explained.

"I know," the mayor replied. "Good luck."

Early the next morning word travelled rapidly around town and across the school district. The town council had raised the governor's ante. In addition to the $3.5 million fewer dollars the town would be getting from the state capital, the council members, despite the pleas from DelVecchio and Maris, had listened to their own auditor. The auditor had determined that the school district was hiding $6.5 million. Therefore, the town council voted to cut the defeated school budget an additional and coincidental $6.5 million.

Mayor Kim smiled as he read the reports online in the local newspaper.

Adding the Governor's and the town council's cuts, the district educating more than 14,000 of Menlo Grove's children would have $10 million less next year. Fuel, medical insurance, and special education mandated costs alone would add an additional $26 million to the district's expenses. That meant DelVecchio and Maris would need to find $36 million just to have the same dollars as the current year to run the town's schools. In addition, the town had lost $50 million in tax ratables as local businesses closed their doors or moved manufacturing overseas. Even with all the cuts, the town would still fall short on the amount of money the school district needed. Mayor Kim knew towns could only raise revenue in one way.

"Wonder how Mayor Ravioli and the town council will pay to run the schools without raising property taxes now?" Mayor Kim asked himself rhetorically.

"And I would love to see DelVecchio try to put together a plan for running the school district with $10 million less," Mayor Kim thought as he smiled to himself.

THIRTY-FOUR

THE UNION BOSS

Menlo Grove Teachers' Association President Kristoff Kaifes sat in his office located in a strip mall along Highway 72. New Board of Education president Larry Griffiths agreed to meet Kaifes to discuss the direction of public education in the town. At least, that's what Griffiths thought. In fact, Kaifes needed to get Griffiths' ear in order to save the jobs of 130 paraprofessionals, all dues paying members of the Menlo Grove Teachers' Association.

"I know we have our differences," Kaifes began, "but we must be able to maintain a professional relationship so we can have a give and take. I owe it to my membership, and you owe it to the taxpayers."

"I am always ready to sit down and talk, Mr. Kaifes," Griffiths began.

"Call me Kristoff."

"Fine, Kristoff. But you must understand, as president of the Board of Education, I do represent the taxpayers, and we are facing a fiscal crisis in Menlo Grove like never before." Griffiths seemed clear and calm.

"Many, many of my membership are taxpayers in Menlo Grove as well, you know," Kaifes countered.

"I am well aware of that, but your membership's candidates lost the last election. The Board needs to find ways to cut many millions of dollars from this budget."

"But, Larry, you can't cut on the backs of our children, especially our special education children." Kaifes could recite the talking points of the union in his sleep.

"You saw and heard those paras and teachers at the last Board meeting. And don't forget the special education parents who spoke."

Griffiths, the oldest member of the Board of Education and retired from his professional career, spent his days at home, and so he had the time to know the numbers he had studied day after day. He was also well aware of the scene at the last Board meeting. The auditorium at the high school was nearly filled with paras, teachers, and parents urging the Board to reconsider the idea of privatizing the paras.

"Kristoff, we both know the real money savings lie in personnel. We have to cut somewhere, and the number of paraprofessionals in this district far outnumbers those in districts nearly our size. We are overstaffed."

"If the district decides to lay off our paras, do you know how many special needs students will go without the assistance we are morally and legally responsible to provide?" Kaifes quickly responded.

"We will meet every child's needs," Griffiths insisted. "We just don't have to do it with district personnel."

"You're making a mistake," Kristoff stated.

"The Board is going the route many other districts have already done. Outsourcing the paraprofessionals is a step in that direction."

"You can't outsource teachers to Asia," Kristoff said, trying to stay focused.

"Of course not. But many local companies are getting themselves well established by offering school districts services the districts used to do themselves. You know, like food service. Many schools used to run their own cafeterias, but most now contract with a food service provider at a lower cost than it used to cost the district to run its own cafeterias."

"That's because those private companies pay the food workers a pittance, and the workers do not belong to a union, and have no collective bargaining rights, and therefore have no job protection," Kaifes declared.

"Welcome to the 21st century," Griffiths smiled.

"So now you're proposing doing the same thing with the paras? Our paras only make about half of what a starting teacher makes. What will your outsourcing company pay them?"

"$11.00 an hour," Griffiths replied calmly.

"They can't live on $11.00 an hour."

"They can't live on what they're being paid now. But the costs of their benefits are killing us. We can't afford it any more," Griffiths said.

"What kind of benefits will workers have if you privatize? What will this company offer them?" Kaifes asked.

"They will be able to purchase some medical benefits and contribute to a pension fund."

"At $11.00 and hour? You're kidding, right? Who would take such a job?" Kaifes seemed to be regaining his confidence.

Griffiths countered, "I sat through Board meeting after meeting listening to para after para explain quite eloquently how they would work for nothing more than the satisfaction they get out of helping our special needs children."

"So that's what you propose to do? Pay them nothing more than the satisfaction of their jobs?"

"No, the company will pay them $11.00 an hour."

"I'm telling you, you won't get anyone to take those jobs," Kaifes insisted.

"In this economy? We'll see," Griffiths countered.

"Yes, we will see. And we'll see you at the next Board meeting. Expect an even bigger crowd of special ed parents."

Griffiths knew he held the upper hand economically, but was also well aware that parents of special education children wanted to hear nothing about economics when it came to educating their child. No Board president wanted hundreds of parents in a dither showing up at a meeting.

"Kristoff, you're over reacting. We have to work out a solution to our budget problems. What do you propose we do?"

"Cut administrators. Cut supervisors. Cut assistant principals."

Griffiths exhaled, "Even if we cut all those positions, we couldn't get close to meeting our budget numbers. And if we did cut those positions, who would make sure the teachers are teaching the Board-approved curriculum and how they are supposed to teach?"

"The teachers don't need watching over. They are professionals."

"I thought this meeting would be more productive," Griffiths conceded.

"I am not going to let you cut into my membership and stay silent."

"We have already sent out notices to all the non-tenured teachers we will not be rehiring due to the budget situation. That cuts into your membership."

"That's different. They don't have tenure. I protect who I can."

Griffiths shook his head and smiled. "I cannot believe the old Board gave para professionals tenure protection. Okay, listen, maybe you and I can come to an agreement. I have to make a public statement at the Board meeting that all the paras must go because of the budget, but in truth, I have concerns with the outsourcing outfit. I am not convinced they are doing due diligence in their hiring practices."

"Fair enough," Kaifes answered. "We will work out a number of paras who get called back, but I have to make some public noise to show support for my rank and file. You're not the only one who has to run for reelection, you know."

"Agreed," Griffiths replied smiling. "But try to keep the special ed parents away from the next meeting. We're going to have enough fireworks as it is."

"I cannot forbid people from attending a public meeting," Kaifes said and, also smiling. "What kind of fireworks?"

"We will be voting on whether Acting Superintendent DelVecchio gets his new contract," Griffiths said. He had stopped smiling.

"Oh, yeah, of course. It's June already. I wonder how that vote will go?" Kaifes looked questioningly at Griffiths.

"Yes, that will be interesting," Griffiths flatly stated.

The phone rang in Kaifes' office.

"Mr. DelVecchio is on the phone," his secretary announced.

"Okay, put him on," Kaifes said.

"Hello, Michael, how are you? I'm good. No, I haven't seen or heard from Larry Griffiths. You know it would be inappropriate for me to meet with him privately."

Kaifes held his hand over the receiver and waved as Larry Griffiths stood up and tiptoed out of the room.

THIRTY-FIVE

THE PRINCIPALS

With June's presence heavy in the big meeting room, the principals arrived at central office for their last formal meeting. Now that the calendar had turned to the cusp of summer, the air conditioning in the central office began ascending as the room temperature descended precipitously. Assistant Superintendent Michael Ferrone still conducted these monthly meetings alone. The new Assistant Superintendent for Student Services had not yet begun working, so there would be no news regarding special education.

The state tests had been given, collected, packed, and returned, so testing coordinator Brenda Dredahl would offer nothing in her report except her usual checklist, delivered staccato style, with a sense of bravado, of minor infractions she had discovered as testing occurred.

During state testing days, Dredahl would meet with the testing coordinator in each building, firing questions of protocol as the harried coordinator tried to keep the testing moving along smoothly despite the late arrivals and absenteeism of students, as well as missing teachers and clueless subs. Dredahl enjoyed walking the halls and poking her head into classrooms while the students sat, heads down, focused on the tests. The principals preferred she just disappear.

Of course, Acting Superintendent DelVecchio usually made an appearance at Ferrone's monthly principals' meetings, but one could never tell when he would suddenly walk through the door or for how long he would stay. Ferrone had gotten used to DelVecchio's long and rambling interruptions as the Acting Superintendent paced while he spoke to the principals.

Ferrone called on Dredahl to issue her testing report. Her arrogant tone was met by the frosty stares from the principals. When Dredahl finished, Ferrone mentioned his reaction to the funeral he had just attended of a beloved district employee. Every principal in the room felt the loss due the recent death of middle school principal Doug Durling. Durling had fought a valiant battle against cancer, coming to work nearly daily despite the chemotherapy and radiation treatments. He had lost his hair and much of the weight from his slender frame, but he never lost his dignity or his warm smile. At his funeral on the previous Saturday morning, the women wept openly and the men wore faces dark as their suits.

Rosemary Grogan-Unangst, elementary principal and she-wolf, raised her hand. Ferrone recognized her and nodded in her direction. The petite and attractive Grogan-Unangst stood and spoke for the group, acknowledging Durling's positive attitude, his never-ending passion, and his enthusiasm for the education of adolescences. She quickly sat back down. Her misting eyes were mimicked by most in the room. Ferrone added how everyone would miss him. Durling, a good man, a life-long public educator, dead at sixty.

Just as Ferrone began reporting on the new budget numbers for textbooks and teacher training, the door of DelVecchio's office opened. Michael DelVecchio entered the large meeting room standing taller than he had seemed in the past six weeks. He wore a sharply tailored gray pin-striped suit, crisp white shirt with gold cufflinks, red and gold tie impeccably tied with the dimple perfectly centered, and loafers shining like a fire truck ready for a Memorial Day parade.

Everyone in the room sat a little straighter. No one was sure whether this would be DelVecchio's last appearance in front of them. The budget battle, the Board election, the slashing of non-tenured teachers, textbooks, and para professionals had taken a toll on every administrator, but DelVecchio bore the burden most of all. His future as an educator would be revealed at the next Board meeting, when the Board would vote on whether or not a new contract would be offered to him.

No one could anticipate what would happen next Monday night when the Board met, but DelVecchio gave the appearance, on this morning at least, that he had an idea. His dignified mien and confident demeanor as he entered the room offered hope to every principal, the exact prescription needed after Durling's recent passing.

Ferrone looked up as DelVecchio walked past him and into the center of the room. The principals sat around DelVecchio, looking up at him like kindergartners on the first day of school. As usual, DelVecchio got right to the point.

"Many of you have heard a lot of rumors about my future," he began. "But let me tell you right here and right now. I am going nowhere. I will see Menlo Grove through this budget crisis. The new Board members are seeing they need a stable hand to guide the district through this difficult time."

He smiled to himself, as if he knew something no one else in the room knew. "Even our new Board president is realizing it is much easier to criticize fellow Board members and second guess the superintendent when you're just a Board member sitting at the far end of the dais. When you become Board president and have to make decisions, second guessing is not quite as simple." DelVecchio smiled again.

Some of the principals also smiled and shook their heads in agreement. " I don't want anyone in this room to worry about me. I am going to be fine, and I will continue to work with each of you here to see to it that Menlo Grove offers its students the best education in the state."

While most in attendance kept nodding in agreement, a few principals stopped smiling and looked at one another. Had DelVecchio forgotten the district's frightening lack of technology, its crumbling buildings, the more than 100 teachers sent home due to lack of funds, the nearly 150 paraprofessionals without jobs and the hundreds of special needs students without aides?

"The Board is considering bringing back the paras," DelVecchio offered. The principals sat even straighter and leaned forward.

"Where will they find the money?" Cyndi Zubricki asked timidly.

"The Board believes we may be overstaffed with supervisors," he replied.

An audible groan rose from the room.

"How do we supervise teachers without supervisors?" Zubricki followed up without irony.

"That's your job," DelVecchio answered. "You're all experts in your field.

Scott Perrillo appealed, "Michael, I manage a building; I'm not a curriculum expert. I need my supervisor, and most importantly, my teachers need the supervisor."

DelVecchio waved his hand in deference. "You will do just fine. The Board listened to the protests of the paras and the parents of the special education students at the last Board meeting. The Board is reconsidering what to do with the paras. In addition, a large number of teachers expressed that they don't think the supervisors are necessary."

All the principals' eyes rolled up into their heads. Even Jimmy Bede raised his eyebrows a little.

"I am just saying the Board is reconsidering. No decisions have been made yet." DelVecchio looked around the room.

"If there are no other questions, I look forward to seeing you next Monday night at the Board meeting. Thank you."

As quickly as he had appeared, DelVecchio disappeared through the doorway entering into his office. The principals looked dumbly at Ferrone. He returned the look.

Ferrone quickly reviewed the textbook strategy for the next year. The supervisors had devised a plan for one year to limit textbook overlap and the use of out of date copies. Ferrone oversaw and agreed to the plan with only minor modifications. The complete elimination of funding for teacher training meant the supervisors also would lead the training based on their content area of expertise. The supervisors would be kept busy next year, and right now it looked like there might be fewer of them keeping busy.

At the conclusion of the meeting, the principals wandered out of the room, a bit like they had just walked blindly into a bathroom door at 2:00 A.M. DelVecchio's confident demeanor had quickly dissipated during the few minutes following his departure. No one knew what would occur at Monday's Board of Ed meeting. Uncertainty was an educator's bane. Teachers survived because they always had a plan and a back up plan. But right here, right now, no one knew. No one knew.

As Ferrone organized his papers in the emptied room, he noticed Rosemary Grogan-Unangst sitting alone. She held her head with her left hand. Ferrone approached her. He may not have trusted her, but he liked her nonetheless. She was a superb educator.

"You okay, Rosemary?" he asked.

"Upset about these cuts. So many young teachers gone. Some of our best and brightest."

"Well, not all," Ferrone offered. "I've read all of the evaluations from your building of Maureen Maddox. You must be happy she is not being renewed. Those evaluations of her teaching were horrible."

Grogan-Unangst's face firmed and her eyes, burning in anger, now stared straight at Ferrone.

"We're keeping her," she said through clenched teeth.

"What? No way. Her evaluations were terrible."

"I said we're keeping her," she repeated, suddenly standing up and collecting her materials. "DelVecchio told me we're keeping her."

"But why?" Ferrone asked.

Rosemary stopped at the door and turned to face Ferrone.

"Because her father is a fucking cop in town. That's why," she said, spinning on her heels and leaving Ferrone alone, mouth agape, in the large, desolate, and freezing cold room.

THIRTY-SIX

THE BOARD OF EDUCATION

People began filling in the seats in the Menlo Grove South auditorium an hour before the 7:30 Board of Education meeting starting time. Normally, anyone attending a Board of Education meeting could show up at any time and have an array of choice seating. Not tonight. Tonight the Board of Education would vote on which budget items would be cut in order to meet the $10 million shortfall. In addition, the Board would vote to determine whether Michael DelVecchio would be offered a new contract, finally granting him the title of Superintendent rather than Acting Superintendent.

By 7:15 every seat in the auditorium was filled, and people arriving after that began to stand along the side aisles and in the back of the large room. Board president Larry Griffiths decided to begin the meeting a few minutes early as the crowd already seemed loud and potentially unruly.

About 60% of those in the audience wore red T-shirts, signifying their support for the Menlo Grove Teachers' Association. Another 20% mixed in the blanket of red were parents of special education students, interested in whether their children would keep the personal aide they knew, or whether someone from the privatization plan and making $11 an hour would assist the children during the day.

The remainder of the audience contained retirees concerned about property taxes and propelled off their couches by pension envy. The district administrators, directors, and supervisors sat in the front right section of the auditorium, dressed in the suits and dresses they had worn to work that day.

By the time the public portion of the meeting occurred, the line of speakers at the podium and microphone stretched all the way up the left aisle to the rear doorway, and wound around the back of the room. Former Board president Bill Burton stood and counted the number of people in line. He sat and raised his hand to be recognized by Larry Griffiths.

After being given the floor, Burton leaned toward the microphone in front of him while looking sideways at Griffiths. "There are sixty-one people in line waiting to speak. The Board rule allows six minutes per speaker. Mr. President, if every speaker takes the full six minutes, that's, let me see, uh, 366 minutes. Divided by 60 minutes per hour. That's over six hours. We are looking at over six hours of questions and comments from the public."

Some clapping and some booing rose from the crowd. The administrators, supervisors, and directors groaned.

"What is your point, Mr. Burton?" Griffiths asked.

"Mr. Griffiths, I propose we limit the speakers to two minutes, and no speaker can ask more than one question."

The majority of the audience booed.

Vita Viterelli immediately spoke, "I second Mr. Burton's proposal."

The booing grew in volume.

"Okay," Griffiths said, looking warily at the crowd. "The proposal is that speakers will be limited to two minutes with no follow up questions. Mr. Maris, take the roll."

Dan Maris read each board member's name and recorded the member's vote. The proposal passed unanimously.

The booing, more intense at first, subsided like a spent wave returning to the sea.

Everyone settled in for two hours of questions and comments from the public.

Nearly an hour of complaints and rhetorical questions followed. A para that had cared for twelve-year-old boy for the past six years spoke about her daily responsibilities with this student. Confined to a wheelchair, blind, unable to speak, and mentally challenged, the boy was fed, cleaned, toileted, and massaged by the aide. The aide wept as she described how a 60% cut in salary and a 100% cut in benefits would not allow her to continue caring for this student.

A parent of another special education student shot a series of rhetorical questions at the Board, not allowing time for an answer, even if any of the questions could be answered. "Do you expect these children to care for themselves?" "You people don't get it, do you?" "Are you kidding me?"

Cheers or hoots, sometimes both, met each speaker's words. The crowd overwhelmingly favored the educators, but the retired taxpayers, comfortable and under the influence of their prescription drugs paid for by the federal government, held up their end in the noise and sarcasm departments.

A man in his early forties, dressed in khakis and blue pullover golf shirt, stepped up to the podium and gave his name and address. No one seemed to know him. His soft polite tone belied his passion. "I have been waiting in line for an hour listening to well-intentioned paraprofessionals, parents of special education students, and teachers speak in protest about the cutting or outsourcing of the aide position. As important as that position is, I am surprised that not one person has spoken against the cutting of full-day kindergarten."

Two people in the rear of the auditorium clapped. "When Menlo Grove cuts full day kindergarten to half day, our students' education is cut by more than half, minute-wise. Why has the Board decided to reconsider putting paraprofessionals back into the budget, but not full-day kindergarten? The cost of reinstating twenty-some kindergarten teachers is far less than the cost of over 100 paras. However, the cost to our children's education is incalculable."

Griffiths leaned into his microphone. "We have received almost no complaints about cutting kindergarten to half-day."

"Does the Board make educational decisions based on the loudest voices or on data and research?"

The Board faced another rhetorical question they cared not to answer.

The man at the podium continued, "Well, I don't know what 'almost no complaints means,' but let me offer my complaint. The Board is being shortsighted in this decision. Early childhood education is the key to school success. And besides, what do you propose I do with my five-year old for half a day? Both my wife and I work."

The snickers softly rolled around the room. The dad, so concerned with early childhood education, had revealed his real reason for full day kindergarten had to do with his and his wife's work schedules. The members of the Board relaxed. Griffiths thanked the man, and assured him no final decisions would be made until later tonight.

The line of red-shirted paras and teachers continued. Several parents spoke emotionally about what the change in paraprofessional would mean to their child. A few of the retired regulars regurgitated their usual rebuttals to those who spoke for not cutting personnel.

Barbara Jean Cox, elementary school principal, stood next in last in line. Sometimes, teachers who resided in town spoke during the public portion of the meeting, but administrators almost never did. B.J. gave her name and address, and took out a written manuscript.

"I am here tonight to speak for the continued leadership of Michael DelVecchio, our much loved Acting Superintendent of schools. Mr. DelVecchio has given over forty years of dedicated leadership and loyalty to the Menlo Grove Public Schools. It is my sincere hope, and I know I speak for many in this audience tonight, that the Board of Education names Michael DelVecchio as Superintendent. Not to do so would be a disgrace; it would rip the hearts out of our schools; it would interrupt his outstanding leadership. Please, members of the Board, appoint Mr. DelVecchio as our superintendent. Please do so for our children. Thank you."

Many in the crowd cheered lustily while others clapped politely.

Finally, at 10:02 P.M. the final person in line stood at the podium and removed the microphone from its stand and held it in his hand like a lounge singer. Association president Kristoff Kaifes, who always spoke last, turned to the audience.

"I want to thank everyone who spoke tonight for the children of Menlo Grove."

He turned now to face the Board of Education. "And I sincerely hope the members of the Board, especially the newest members, have heard what the public had to say."

He turned his back to the Board and spoke again directly to the crowd in the auditorium.

"The people in this room tonight spoke for the students who could not be here."

"Mr. Kaifes, Mr. Kaifes," Larry Griffiths spoke with irritation. "Please face the Board and address the president. This is no time for making a speech."

Kaifes turned again, somewhat bemused. "Of course, Mr. Griffiths. I just hope you and the other members of the Board have listened and have kept an open mind."

"I can assure you we have, Mr. Kaifes." "

Kaifes was not done.

"I also feel I must speak on behalf of Acting Superintendent Michael DelVecchio. As we all know, his current contract expires at the end of the month, and I hope and pray... I hope and I pray that the Board will offer Mr. DelVecchio a new contract and name him Superintendent, a title he so richly deserves."

A great number of people in the audience, including most of the administrators, applauded.

"Thank you." Griffiths, himself bemused, looked at the large crowd. "Because of the large number of speakers tonight, I am directing that we take a short break before moving forward with tonight's agenda. Ten minutes. Thank you."

With that, the members of the audience rose as if a very long church service had just concluded. The noise level rose, and people stretched, moaned, and debriefed with the neighbors. A large percentage of the red-shirted crowd immediately left for the exits. School would beckon in the early morning. They had made their presence and point.

The meeting restarted twenty minutes later. The auditorium, now half-filled, had lost the vast majority of its red-shirted attendees. Those representing the administrators and supervisors sat wearily in the front, anxious for things to get going so they could get going home.

Larry Griffiths softly banged the gavel to bring the remaining crowd to order. Immediately past president Bill Burton raised his hand to be recognized.

"Yes, Mr. Burton?" Griffiths said.

"I would like to make a motion that the Board approve Michael DelVecchio as Superintendent," Burton declared.

"Right now?" Griffiths asked. "We still have many other agenda items to address."

"And what is more important than knowing whether or not Mr. DelVecchio will continue leading the district?"

Griffiths looked down the dais at the other members. They all stared straight back at him.

Vito Viterelli spoke up, "I second Mr. Burton's proposal."

Griffiths looked at Board attorney Bob Butterfield. "Should I take a vote on whether we take a vote?" he asked.

Butterfield shrugged his shoulders. Griffiths called for a vote to vote. Dan Maris called the roll. The vote to vote was unanimous.

"What did we just vote on?" new Board member Laura Benderman asked.

Board president Griffiths answered, "Uh, we just voted to vote on Mr. DelVecchio's new contract."

"But of course we have to vote on it." She stated. "Mr. DelVecchio's contract ends in ten days. We have to make a decision."

"Wait a minute," interrupted long-time Board member Vito Viterelli. 'I didn't know that's what we were voting on."

"Maybe we should re-vote," Board president Griffiths offered, looking over at Board attorney Butterfield.

The remaining crowd in the audience simultaneously groaned and roared with rude laughter.

"The Board can now vote on the proposal to offer Mr. DelVecchio a new contract," Butterfield announced.

"Okay." Griffiths said. "We are going to vote on the recommendation that Mr. DelVecchio be named Superintendent of the Menlo Grove Public Schools."

The audience, sensing something finally was about to happen, sat up.

The administrators in the front rows awoke from their slumber. Ferrone sat next to Lucy Williams. He leaned over and whispered to her, "Watch the three new members seated all the way at the far end of the dais. DelVecchio only has three sure yes votes: Burton, Viterelli, and Casella. Steinmetz is a wild card. He needs one of those new people to vote yes, or he has to hope he has moved Griffiths to the yes column as well."

"Oh, really?" Williams declared. "I hadn't realized that. Wait, I think I'm confused."

Ferrone also seemed confused that people, like Lucy, could get so caught up in their actual work they missed the politics of the place.

"If all three of the new members vote no, DelVecchio is gone," he clarified.

"Oh, my," Williams exclaimed. "I would hate that. I really don't like change."

Ferrone rolled his eyes and listened and Business Administrator and Board Secretary Dan Maris took the roll call vote. The three new members would vote first.

"Ms. Benderman?"

"No."

"Mrs. Wichniczak?"

"No."

Lucy Williams suddenly grabbed Ferrone's forearm.

There was one more remaining new member, Asshiyani Gupta, whose friend DelVecchio had named new Assistant Superintendent of Student Services.

"Mrs. Gupta?"

"No."

Lucy Williams made a slightly audible "Oh, no." About two dozen others in the auditorium also made unrecognizable sounds.

The vote continued.

"Mrs. Casella?"

"Yes."

"That's one," Ferrone thought as Lucy Williams eased her grip on his arm somewhat.

"Mr. Viterelli?"

"Yes."

"Mr. Burton?"

"Yes."

The vote now stood at 3-3. DelVecchio needed two of the three remaining votes. The audience leaned forward. Ferrone's eyes widened.

"Mrs. Steinmetz?"

"Yes."

Now the noise from the audience became more than audible. Some cheers could be heard.

"Ms. Szygieski?"

"No."

Four votes in favor of extending DelVecchio's contract, four votes opposing.

One more member needed to vote - newly elected Board president Larry Griffiths.

"Mr. Griffiths?"

All present held their breaths. Had DelVecchio's bending over backward, buying Griffiths lunch, and agreeing to cuts against what DelVecchio truly believed, manage to win over the new Board president's vote? DelVecchio looked down at the table and closed his eyes.

"No."

Maris read the results. "The vote to appoint Mr. DelVecchio as superintendent is 5-4 opposed. The vote fails."

The color from Maris's face disappeared. He looked up from the paper he held in his hand and blinked twice.

Cheers and boos rose from the remaining audience.

"Oh, my God," Lucy Williams cried.

"Holy shit," shouted Barbara Jean Cox.

Larry Griffiths pounded the gavel. "Order, please."

DelVecchio called for the microphone. Griffiths, clearly confused, handed it to him.

DelVecchio cleared his cigarette-clogged throat.

"I just want to say that this Board has made a big mistake tonight."

Applause came from some of the remaining crowd, including many of the administrators.

"No one will be able to move this district forward except me," DelVecchio declared. "I have more experience and knowledge of this community than anyone. I cannot be replaced. The Board...the Board...."

He stopped, not sure what else to say. He swallowed and looked bewildered. Then he stood up and quickly began walking up the far aisle leading to the exit.

Suddenly, Ferrone found himself sitting amidst a rustling of butts, legs, and pocketbooks. The administrators and supervisors surrounding Ferrone had stood and were leaving. Ferrone looked around, trying to catch someone's eye, but everyone around him seemed determined to get out of that auditorium right now.

Within seconds, Ferrone sat almost alone in the front section of the auditorium. Three rows ahead of him he spotted testing coordinator Brenda Dredahl still seated, staring straight ahead, eyes glazed.

Ferrone looked back to Board president Griffiths. Board members Vito Viterelli and Bill Burton had disappeared from their seats at the dais. Apparently, they too had walked out. The Board now had only seven members present.

Some of those remaining in the auditorium stood and jeered.

Larry Griffiths stood at the dais, observing the chaos. Board attorney Bob Butterfield leaned over and softly asked Griffiths, "What will you do now for a superintendent?"

"Not to worry," Griffiths said, smiling smugly. "I know a guy who knows a guy."

EPILOGUE

GRADUATION

High school English teacher Leonia Calabrese led the graduation procession of the senior class out of the high school, into the sun and onto the green grass of the football field. When she arrived at the foot of the stage, located on the goal line, she smiled up at principal Grace Romanczak.

Grace, dressed in green graduation gown, stood on the stage. Leonia stepped aside and watched as the seniors filled row after row of folding chairs placed along every other yard line. She sat only after giving the signal and waiting for every twelfth grader to sit in unison.

Leonia sat on the end of row 1, constantly keeping her head at a ninety-degree angle from the stage, so she could be on constant watch for a beach ball or other disruptive distraction coming from the students. Acting Superintendent DelVecchio, in his last official appearance, stood at the podium and greeted the seniors and their parents, grandparents, and friends. He then turned to Board president Larry Griffiths, announced that the class had met all the requirements for a high school diploma, walked down the steps of the stage, onto the green lushness of the field, through the center aisle separating the twenty-five rows of students, and out of the stadium. No one seemed to know what was going on. The head of a school district always offered a few

congratulatory words and then sat through the entire cere-
mony, often shaking the hand of each graduate as the smiling young person received the diploma. Leonia Calabrese
watched quizzically as DelVecchio passed her and the rest
of the graduates. He chose to skip all of this.

"If I live to be 100," Calabrese thought to herself, "I'll
never figure out just what goes on in that central office."

The Supervisor – By mid-July, people working in the central office noticed that elementary supervisor Lucy Williams
had not been to work in two weeks. Although many of the
staff took vacation time in early July, Lucy had not submitted paper work stating her summer vacation dates. Twelve-
month employee contract language stated twenty-five
days of vacation per year. Those who retired with unused
vacation time earned a per diem stipend for each unused
day. A phone call from big-haired secretary Bertha Butz to
Lucy's home found that Lucy's husband had not heard from
her either. He assumed she was staying in Menlo Grove with
friends, as she did with more and more frequency to avoid
both the long commute and her husband. Lucy the supervisor had disappeared. Eventually, secretary Butz received
a post card from Lucy. Seems the young girl who feared
abandonment, and the woman who perfected silence to
avoid it, had abandoned both her personal and professional lives. She told no one that she had electronically submitted retirement papers with the state on the last day of
June and caught a plane departing the state's largest air-
port the next morning at 6:17 A.M. The message written on
the post card Bertha Butz received stated, "The only thing I
ever wanted was to be happy. And now I am." It was post-
marked from the Cayman Islands.

The Assistant Superintendent – Lilly Laboy had completed
the first six months of her retirement working for the school
district and she still wore many hats: legal coordinator of
the tenure case; private advisor and confidante to the acting superintendent; ghost writer for DelVecchio of yearly

evaluations; vote counter for controversial issues facing the Board. Though most of the Board members did not know that Laboy still had a loud voice in district procedures, each month she was paid on a per diem basis that the Board approved under the account labeled "Miscellaneous Expenses." After her last meeting with DelVecchio, when he indirectly blamed her for the sudden and embarrassing resignation of Abha Patel, she decided to spend all of her days at the Shore with her husband, and began a part time job doing inventory and as general salesperson for an upscale child's boutique located near the ocean. She could not remember ever being happier. Within a year of her retirement, some people in Menlo Grove remembered her name and work ethic, how she had changed once she left working in a school building and moved to the central office, but very few could recall any positive influence she had on the district.

The New Guy – Following the Board election in April, Michael Ferrone began to consider walking away from public education. His extensive years as a classroom teacher and supervisor in no way prepared him for the decision-making process of the central office which was based first and foremost on political considerations. His career path had followed three simple guidelines that had served him well: 1- learn something new every day; 2- laugh while at work at least once a day; 3- make a difference. The years in the classroom and supervising other teachers had made those three rules easy to attain. His time in the central office had made those guidelines moot. While he had written his letter of intent to resign and retire almost immediately after the Board election, he waited to submit it until one of the very few days DelVecchio had come to work following the last Board meeting in June. He asked DelVecchio's secretary early one morning if he could see the outgoing Acting Superintendent. The secretary informed Ferrone that Mr. DelVecchio would be leaving as soon as his current phone call ended. Before returning to his office, Ferrone put on his game face, looked the secretary directly in the eyes, and firmly said he needed to talk to DelVecchio and it was urgent. Minutes later, DelVecchio stood at the door of Ferrone's office. Ferrone could not recall if this was the first time the Acting Superintendent had ever been in Ferrone's office. Ferrone got to the point quickly.

"Here is my letter of resignation with intent to retire."

DelVecchio looked quickly at the document and quickly sat down. Ferrone had finally gotten the old man's attention.

"How many years you got in?" DelVecchio asked while staring at the letter.

"Thirty-five."

"I didn't know that," DelVecchio stated. "Are you sure?"

Ferrone wondered if he was being asked if he was sure of his decision to retire or if he was sure he had been in education for thirty-five years.

"Yes, I am sure."

DelVecchio refolded the letter, looked down at his hands, and suddenly stood up, and walked out of Ferrone's office, exiting the side door of the building. It was the last time Ferrone ever saw him.

The Interview Committee – When DelVecchio decided to forego interview committees and began making hiring decisions based solely on political considerations, he was following a long history of top down management. Following DelVecchio's retirement, the subsequent superintendent decided he would not follow the DelVecchio model. He went DelVecchio one better. He decided to meet selected candidates before allowing any candidate to meet the interview committees, thereby becoming his own one-man screening committee. No one got to the committee unless the superintendent already had approved the candidate first.

The Acting Superintendent – Michael DelVecchio spent years and most of his energy maintaining a grip on his position and trying to garner a new contract as superintendent. His disregard for the expertise of his subordinates, and his decisions based on what he thought would help him continue his career, turned out to be in vain. In the end, he had forgotten one of the basic tenets of coaching: you cannot win if you play not to lose. His vivacious wife Concetta joined him in retirement as she left her position as a high school math teacher. They moved to a warmer and tax-friendlier state in order to be closer to their children and grandchildren. Six months after graduation, DelVecchio had quit smoking, lost twenty pounds, and while his golf game did not improve much, how much he enjoyed playing increased immeasurably.

The Mayor's Office – Mayor Kim assisted in the transition to Mayor-elect Rosie Ravioli, who easily won election as the first woman mayor of Menlo Grove. Ravioli was in office for nine months when she made drastic cuts in the number of town employees, their pensions, and payouts at retirement. The police and fire fighter unions immediately began a petition for a recall election.

The Union Boss – Kristoff Kaites won reelection as president of the Menlo Grove Teachers' Association, beating back a challenge from a high school Phys.Ed. teacher, who was upset with the low pay of the coaches' stipends. Kaifes promised to limit the number of lay offs and hold the line on give backs during the next contract negotiations. After two years of working without a contract, Kaifes and his negotiating team finally agreed to settle on a three-year contract where the teacher salaries were set at -1%, 0%, and +1.0%. In addition, teachers would pay 30% of their medical insurance, an average of about $6,000 per teacher. Overall, teachers would end the next three years making less money than they had when the previous contract began. Kaifes submitted his resignation and retirement paperwork the day after the new contract was signed and before the agreements in the new contract took effect. Forty-nine of fifty eligible staff members in the district immediately retired. Only elementary principal Jimmy Bede decided to return for his fifty-first year.

The Principals – In mid-October, Jimmy Bede failed to come out of his office to eat lunch with the third grade students, something he did daily. His secretary found Jimmy dead at his desk. Autopsy reports showed Jimmy had choked to death on a chocolate chip cookie. Two of the three she-wolves retired during the following year, each submitting her paperwork the day of her fifty-fifth birthday. Only Rosemary Grogan-Unangst remained behind. Because she had taken off twelve years to raise her children, she still had to work three more years before reaching twenty-five years. After twenty-five years, a public educator received free medical benefits for life. However, during the three remaining years Rosemary worked, the legislature changed the early retire-ment age from 55 to 60, and instead of free medical care, retirees now had to pay a portion of the income toward that insurance. The change from age 55 to 60 cost Rosemary more than $6000 each year. The insurance cost her another $6000 every year. The Governor signed the legislation and complained loudly that retired teachers who listened to their union leaders were "idiot dirt bags" and would still be "getting away with murder because of their lucrative pen-sions and benefits." It was a cruel and calculated political exploitation played on those who dedicated their working careers teaching children to read, to calculate, and to be honest and responsible.

The Board of Education – Board president Larry Griffiths pre-sided over a split group of Board of Education members; however his majority stayed solid throughout the follow-ing school year. His three new members and Board vice president gave him a working majority. Margie Steinmetz voted with the majority on most issues. The following spring,

Carla Casella decided not to run for her seat again. Former president Bill Burton, and former V.P. Vito Viterelli were both defeated in their reelection bids. Barely more than twelve months after the decision not to offer Michael DelVecchio a new contract, every one of DelVecchio's supporters was gone from the Menlo Grove Board of Education. The local 14% of registered voters who cast ballots in the school election had spoken. This microcosm of democracy illustrated just how quickly a town with small and petty political interests could turn something as vital to democracy as its entire public educational system upside down.

List of Characters

Sam Applegate – principal of Menlo Grove South High School

Jimmy Bede- elementary principal in his 50th year in the job

Laura Benderman – newly elected member of the board of education

Judy Blinkley – teacher and ex-wife of Ron Blinkley

Ron Blinkley – teacher married to Judy Blinkley before marrying Sharon Johansson

Bill Burton – president of board of education

Bob Butterfield – board of education attorney

Bertha Butz – secretary

Leonia Calabrese – high school English teacher

Anne Carillo – elementary school principal

Carla Casella - member of board of education

Barbara Jean Cox – elementary school principal

Roger D'Amico – appointed board member after Tony Martino's sudden resignation

Judy DeCalma – disabled non-tenured teacher not retained

Brenda Dredahl – testing coordinator

Concetta DelVecchio – high school algebra teacher and wife of Michael DelVecchio

Michael DelVecchio – Acting Superintendent of Schools

Doug Durling – middle school principal, struck by cancer

Debbie Duhan – member of board of education

Shirley Eckhardt – supervisor of social studies

Lou Ferrigno – middle school principal

Michael Ferrone – Assistant Superintendent of Curriculum and Instruction who replaces Lily Laboy

Mike Fiorello – supervisor of attendance and security

Gary Geiger – assistant football coach

Grandma Irene – woman who raises elementary supervisor Lucy Williams

Larry Griffiths – member of board of education

Rosemary Grogan-Unangst – elementary school principal
Asshiyani Gupta – newly elected member of the board of education

Jill Hillebrand – head of guidance at Henry Ford High School

Peter Jenson – Director of Building and Grounds
Sharon Johansson – teacher married to Ron Blinkley
Bobby Jones – supervisor of Physical Education and Health

Kristoff Kaifes – president of Menlo Grove Teachers' Association
Mayor Kim – mayor of Menlo Grove

Lily Laboy – Assistant Superintendent of Curriculum & Instruction, then Assistant Superintendent of Student and Special Services
Charles Laboy – husband of Lilly Laboy, retired principal

Maureen Maddox – young teacher whose father serves as a town police officer
Luigi Marinelli – former Superintendent who served as Michael DelVecchio's mentor
Dan Maris – Business Administrator and Board of Education Secretary
Tony Martino – Menlo Grove Deputy Police Chief and member of board of education
Sam Mussina – supervisor of technology

Dan O'Dowd – middle school principal and candidate for Assistant Superintendent of Student Services

Abha Patel – special education teacher chosen as Assistant Superintendent of Special services
Scott Perrillo – elementary principal
Biff Pisano – supervisor of Art and Music

Rosie Ravioli – member of town council intent on replacing Mayor Kim
Grace Romanczak – principal of Henry Ford High School

Suzee Semanski – member of board of education

Claire Smith – Superintendent of Schools, replaced by Michael DelVecchio

Mike Simone – transportation director

Margie Steinmetz – member of board of education

Dina Thomas – English supervisor

Vito Viterelli – vice president of board of education

Daniel Wells – member of board of education

Danny Wells – school custodian and son of board member Daniel Wells

Joey Wells – middle school history teacher and son of board member Daniel Wells

Emily Wichniezak – newly elected member of the board of education

Lucy Williams – supervisor of elementary education

Cyndi Zubricki – elementary school principal